CONTINUING EDUCATION
AT PURDUE UNIVERSITY, 1975–2019

Copyright 2023 by Thomas Robertson.
Printed in the United States of America.

Cataloging-in-Publication data is on file at the
Library of Congress
978-1-61249-939-0 (paperback)
978-1-61249-940-6 (epdf)

Information about individuals, places, events, and
dates has been provided to the extent it is known.

Front cover image—Stewart Center, courtesy of
Purdue University Archives and Special Collections.

CONTINUING EDUCATION

at Purdue University, 1975–2019

Thomas Robertson and Michael Eddy

Purdue University Press / West Lafayette, Indiana

Contents

	Preface	vii
1.	The Big Picture	1
2.	1974–1984	5
3.	1984–1989	11
4.	1989–1998	15
5.	1999–2002	21
6.	2002–2011	27
7.	2011–2015	39
8.	2015–2019	49
	Conclusion	61
	References	63
	Acknowledgments	65
	Appendixes	
	Biographies of Deans and Directors	67
	Executive Memoranda	73
	Traditional Conferences, Special Interest Conferences, and Continuing Education	81
	Events of Interest Held at Purdue, 1974–2019	83
	About the Authors	85

Preface

Continuing education at purdue university, 1975–2019 is intended to provide a follow-up to the monograph written by Dr. Frank K. Burrin after his retirement as director of Purdue Continuing Education in 1984, *Continuing Education at Purdue University: The First Hundred Years (1874–1974)*. Burrin became ill shortly after his retirement, and he was not able to complete his project. His notes were later compiled, edited, and published by Elizabeth Boyd Thompson.

This monograph presents forty-five years of the history of Continuing Education and Conferences at Purdue under the leadership of eight deans and directors.

In our chapters covering the administrations of these leaders, we refer to the department by the names and acronyms that were then current:

Frank Burrin (1975–1984): During his administration, the department was called Continuing Education Administration.

Charles Elliott (1984–1989): While director, the department was called Continuing Education Administration.

Richard Forsythe (1989–1998): Under his leadership, the department was called Continuing Education Administration and Center for Instructional Services.

Philip Swain (1999–2002): During his administration, the department was reorganized, and it was renamed the Office of Instructional Excellence and Lifelong Learning.

Mark Pagano (2002–2011): During his administration, the department was restructured again and became known as the Office of Continuing Education and Conferences.

Mary Sadowski (2011–2015): Under her leadership, the department name was changed to Purdue Extended Campus.

Steve Abel (2015–present): In April 2015, Purdue Conference Division began reporting through Steve Abel and the Office of Engagement

Jon Harbor, executive director of Digital Education (2015–2018) and provost of Purdue Global (2020–present): In April 2015, all functions related to online learning became a unit called Digital Education and reported through Jon Harbor.

As a land-grant college, Purdue University came about as a result of the Morrill Act of 1862. Purdue was established in 1869 with land and money donated by a prominent Lafayette businessman, John Purdue. Purdue was one of the wealthiest businessmen in Indiana (Norberg 2019, 3). Classes began September 16, 1874. The first commencement was held at Purdue on June 17, 1875. There was one graduate, John Harper.

With the university's beginnings in agricultural extension and service, Continuing Education and Conferences have deep roots at Purdue. The following quote from Purdue President Edward C. Elliott, in 1922, is a testament to this philosophy:

As President of Purdue I will not consider that I have met my responsibilities until the leadership and citizenship of the state of Indiana, of whatever class or occupation, continue to recognize that this University is their University; that Purdue University is an integral part of the public school system of the state ever working in its own distinctive and assigned fields; that Purdue is a worthy agency, ever at their disposal for aiding them to meet the needs that determine the happiness, the satisfaction and the ideals of their lives; until there is firmly established among students and teachers and alumni the enduring principle that the daily work of men makes education possible, and that education in turn must make the daily work of men possible and pleasurable. (Burrin 1970, 85–86)

This ideology continued under the leadership of President Fredrick Hovde, as was evidenced when he appointed Charles Lawshe as the dean of extension and adult education in 1958 (Topping 1980, 308). Hovde asked Lawshe to resolve the conflicts between the divisions of adult education (headed by George Davis) and technical extension (headed by Charles Beese). He did so by creating the Division of Conferences and Continuation Services (Topping 1980, 310). This became the official department to administer adult and continuing education programs, and it assumed responsibility to fully support academic faculty in delivering these programs effectively.

1

THE BIG PICTURE

Today more than ever, American society depends on adult education systems to spread information and knowledge, develop skills and shape attitudes. Various forms of adult education now pervade American life, and the belief that education must extend through adulthood has become commonplace.

—*Stubblefield and Keane 1994, xi*

THE TERM *ADULT EDUCATION* HAS MANY MEANINGS AND can be confusing. Programs ranging from literacy for the undereducated to continuing education for professionals are referred to as adult education. The boundaries of adult education are not certain. *At one extreme*, adult education is considered to include all life experiences through which adults learn. *At the other extreme*, it includes only organized learning experiences.

Forms of adult education have evolved over the years in response to changing conditions. Increases in scientific knowledge and technological applications have brought change in work processes and workplace culture. The great experiments of the early and mid-nineteenth century (the mechanics institutes and the lecture movement) spread general knowledge and culture, as did the chautauquas, university extension, and the world fairs of the late nineteenth and early twentieth centuries. In the second decade of the twentieth century, federal legislation created a national system of agricultural education through the Cooperative Extension Service and vocational education through the public schools. An expanded university extension system and urban evening colleges made higher education more readily available, and the explosion of community colleges after the Second World War brought higher education within commuting distance for most adults.

Americans have learned because there was knowledge to master, technology to adapt to, and uncertainties of life to be resolved. They have learned because of an ideology of self-improvement that spoke to the importance of learning and the promise of education for advancement (Stubblefield and Keane 1994, 312).

Adult education in the United States has been and remains a diverse activity. It emerged not as a form of a definable system, such as schooling or higher education, but in the form of definable educative systems. These educative systems ranged from relatively simple systems created by individuals to the more complex organizational systems of family, religious and educational institutions, voluntary and cultural organizations, and the workplace.

The Morrill Acts (passed in 1862 and 1890) founded the land-grant colleges that received the mission of public responsibility and service. Included in this mission was the concept of extension or carrying knowledge out to the people (Bonhomme 1998).

At Purdue, the mission for educating adults took forms that are familiar at most land-grant institutions. Purdue's agricultural extension service provided agricultural training via extension offices in all the state's counties, as well as training in skills areas related to rural homelife and household economy. Its College of Engineering offered professional training to engineers as well as opportunities to complete master's degrees from worksites. As ably described in Frank Burrin's predecessor volume to this history, administration of adult education at Purdue coalesced around the university-level unit called Continuing Education, which would be known variously as Continuing Education Administration, Continuing Education and Conferences, the Office for Instructional Excellence and Lifelong Learning, and Purdue Extended Campus. In all its incarnations, continuing education's role was to facilitate educational outreach through scheduling, marketing, logistics, registration, and financial services; it was also expected to promote and incentivize these activities to academic departments and faculty members.

Continuing education was part of the university's academic mission and usually reported through the provost. But it was also part of the university's outreach mission and has at times reported through the Office of Engagement. For several years it had a dual reporting line, to both the provost and Engagement. In the reorganization of 2015, the academic portion of continuing education, then called Digital Education, remained with the provost and the conference operation moved to the Office of Engagement. In 2018 Purdue Online became a direct report to the president's office.

Continuing education programming assumed familiar forms as well. Traditional credit courses were offered off campus, on campus at nontraditional hours, and through media-delivery, eventually becoming dominated by online delivery. In addition, advanced degrees, offered remotely to working professionals, were coordinated through continuing education. Noncredit enrichment and professional courses were also offered. A major element in Purdue's outreach education has been conferences held on campus or at remote sites. These have been oriented to professional development, research and scholarship, and enrichment.

The Early Continuing Education Experience at Purdue

Although the Agricultural Experiment Station at Purdue University had been funded by provisions of the Hatch Act in 1887, it was not until 1905 that the Indiana legislature provided funds for the Experiment Station under terms of the Smith Act of 1905. The same year, an Agricultural Extension Department was established as a unit of the Experiment Station. Dr. George I. Christie joined the staff that year to work in the extension areas. He was in charge of Agricultural Extension from 1907 to 1928. One of his first assignments was to organize a new approach to extension—to reach rural Indiana by train. Educational trains made it possible for agricultural extension to reach large numbers of people in a short period of time. This became a cooperative venture between the railroads, Purdue, and local communities that would last nearly fifty years. Fourteen rail systems cooperated with Purdue with no costs to the university. From 1905 to 1937, education trains reached nearly four hundred thousand people at station stops around the state. Subjects covered by the exhibit trains included: corn, dairy, horticulture, soils, wheat, onions, alfalfa, livestock, poultry, marketing, fruits and vegetables, swine, sanitation, lime, legumes, muck crops, and farm/home (Burrin 1988, 15–16).

Additionally, Purdue radio station WBAA received its license to operate on April 4, 1922 (Shipp 2018, 1–2). They broadcast engineering and agriculture classes in the early years. Professors would go on the air from the WBAA studio and students could tune in and listen to lectures. In the 1950s the station became heavily involved in the School of the Air, a state project that was providing programming for public schools. Many of these programs were produced by Richard Forsythe, who would become a director of continuing education later in his career. Under Forsythe's direction, Purdue courses continued to air on WBAA into the 1990s.

From 1960 to 1968, Purdue played a key role in a regional initiative designed to broadcast top-notch educational courses to schools in an era before satellite television or public broadcasting. It was called the Midwest Program on Airborne Television Instruction (MPATI). The initiative used airplanes to broadcast videotaped courses to schools in a six-state area. President Fredrick Hovde supported this program and offered IMPATI executives use of Purdue-owned aircraft as well as university administrative resources (Purdue News Service, 2014b). When MPATI began broadcasting in the fall of 1961, the videotaped courses included social studies, science, language arts, government, math, music, French, Russian, and Spanish. However, the costs associated with MPATI were high. In 1968 MPATI's executive board decided it could no longer afford to produce and broadcast courses.

A fuller accounting of this history is presented in Burrin's *Continuing Education at Purdue University: The First Hundred Years (1874–1974)*, now available online at no charge from Purdue Archives at https://docs.lib.purdue.edu/continuinged/1/.

Where We Begin

The preceding historical summary brings us to the point where the narrative of this monograph begins, with the administration of Frank Burrin starting in 1974. Burrin's history discusses this era somewhat obliquely, perhaps too modestly, and without the perspective of hindsight.

The impact of Burrin's contributions became clearer as the decades passed, even as the lived details were lost. It should be noted that neither of the authors worked under Burrin; we knew him only as a retiree who turned up occasionally at the office to work on his history project. Consequently, our chapter on Burrin's administration is based more on administrative records and secondhand accounts than on the lived experience that we had in the administrations of every other director or dean discussed here.

The monograph ends not with the end of the mission of extended learning, but with a rather radical transformation of how it would be delivered. Conveniently, that transformation corresponded roughly with the retirements of both authors after thirty-plus-year careers in continuing education at Purdue. The narrative we present here is not about the grand sweep of ideas about adult education and extension. It is a ground-level account of how that mission was carried out in the complex, ever-changing environment of a great land-grant university. It is a history of advances and setbacks, of successes that run their course and fade out, of conflicting priorities, and of varying conceptions of how continuing education would fit in the university. It is the nuts and bolts of trying to make the extension mission work in a multifaceted institution. You can, however, hear the shifting of big ideas stirring in the background—how the university comes to recognize that serving a broader base of learners works to its long-term benefit and how technology can be leveraged to efficiently deliver higher education learners everywhere. It is ultimately a success story in which the marginal but plucky enterprise of continuing education eventually comes to be a vital element of the university's growth and success.

2

1974–1984

FRANK BURRIN BECAME DIRECTOR OF CONTINUING Education Administration in 1975. Burrin's professional relationship with Purdue had begun in 1952 when he returned to the university after earning a master's degree in 1947 and then teaching in public schools for five years. While a graduate student, he was hired as a conference coordinator in 1954. He became director of Summer Sessions and Evening Classes in 1962 and director of Conferences and Continuation Services in 1965. He was associate dean under Earl Butz and Charles Lawshe, upon whose retirement in 1975 he became director of Continuing Education Administration. (Burrin was not given the title of dean, which Butz and Lawshe had, because of a new university policy by which only academic areas would have deans.) Burrin held that title until his retirement in 1984 (Burrin 1988, iii–iv).

As director, Burrin reported to Assistant Provost Don Brown. During Burrin's tenure, Brown would rise to the position of vice president and dean of academic services, with oversight of Continuing Education Administration, the Office of Instructional Services, the Office of Instructional Materials Development, the Office of Special Academic Services, the Telecommunication Center, radio station WBAA, Teacher Education Services, the Computing Center, Purdue Libraries, and Audio/Visual Services. Brown would prove to be a powerful ally for Continuing Education and a creative advocate for lifelong learning, as will be shown.

By 1962, Burrin had risen from the role of conference coordinator to director of evening classes and summer sessions. In 1961 he had also been appointed as one of six state regional managers with responsibility for adult learning programs in thirteen counties around Lafayette. In 1965 he was named director of Conferences and Continuing Services and became associate dean of Continuing Education in 1968. As associate dean, Burrin had participated in the establishing of the Dean's Reserve Fund, which allowed Continuing Education to carve out some program revenues to create a fund that could support start-up programs. Burrin had also proposed that Purdue adopt the use of the national Continuing Education Unit for noncredit programs (Burrin 1988, iii).

As Burrin assumed the directorship, the Purdue Board of Trustees resolved on May 10, 1974, that "it is the policy of Purdue to maximize and to extend options to the citizens [of Indiana] to pursue lifelong learning in a variety of formats and that Purdue has a clear charge and role in the area of continuing education." The trustees formed a reorganization task force to extend their vision that continuing education should be an integral part of the university's total educational program (Burrin 1988, 55–56).

Program Status under Burrin

A rough way to assess Burrin's tenure as a whole is to compare the levels of program activity in the academic year before Burrin's directorship, AY 1973–74, to his final complete year, AY 1983–84, as recorded in those years' CEA annual reports.

- The scope of Conferences remained roughly the same: 406 programs with 78,388 attendees in 1973–74 and 425 programs and 80,039 in 1983–84. This variation is well within the normal ebb and flow of Purdue conference business.
- Evening Classes suffered a substantial decline, from 208 classes with 4,644 enrollments in 1973–74 to 89 classes with 1,671 enrollments in 1983–84. This decline may reflect the financial challenges Evening Classes faced (which are discussed in subsequent chapters), an emphasis on other modes of course delivery, and the impact of Ivy Tech. The statewide community/technical college established its Lafayette campus in 1977 and immediately began offering courses that working people needed at times they could attend and at a price substantially lower than Purdue's. Obviously, Ivy Tech's entrance into the market would cut into Purdue's audience substantially.
- By contrast, Extension Classes (Purdue classes taught away from the campus in local facilities) grew significantly, from 27 classes and 1,222 enrollments in 1973–74 to 180 classes and 2,533 enrollments in 1983–84. This reflects a broadening of the sites being used, but also foreshadows a problem Extension Classes would face. Average class size in 1973–74 was 45 students; average class in 1983–84 was 14. Extension classes operated on a self-supporting financial model: each class was expected to meet all its expenses, including instructional costs and administrative costs for the university and for Continuing Education. That is easy to accomplish with 45 students but challenging with 14.
- Courses delivered by media, radio and TV, grew as well. In 1973–74, there were 27 courses taught, with 1,222 enrolled, while in 1983–84, there were 75 courses with 12,149 learners. Radio courses were offered via Purdue's radio station WBAA, and televised courses were offered on channels made available by the Greater Lafayette Cable System. Media-delivered credit courses were offered as credit by examination. Along with Continuing Engineering Education closed-circuit televised courses offered through the Indiana Higher Education Telecommunications System (IHETS), these programs constituted Purdue's early involvement in distance learning.
- Special Summer Courses were credit courses that Continuing Education had been authorized to offer outside the traditional summer eight-week term. These grew very substantially under Burrin's direction, from 25 courses and 383 enrollments in 1973–74 to 90 classes and 1,636 enrollments in 1983–84. In 1982 these classes would morph into Maymester, the popular four-week interim term that was administered by Continuing Education for many years.
- Continuing Education also housed several self-supporting units offering discipline-specific noncredit training to professionals. Those had peaked at the end of Burrin's tenure and included the Insurance Marketing Institute; the Restaurant, Hotel, and Institutional Management Institute; the Retail Institute; the Supervision Institute; and Economic Education. In 1973–74 these units offered 97 programs that enrolled 3,122 participants; in 1983–84 they offered 152 programs with 8,512 enrollments. Despite the institutes' robust development in the 1970s and 1980s, with competition from private consultants and professional associations and

the retirements of the institutes' original entrepreneurial leaders, these units faded in the 1990s and 2000s.

Over Burrin's decade of directing Continuing Education, the annual programs conducted grew from 791 to 1,033, and annual enrollments grew from 89,060 to 110,340. These enrollment numbers placed Purdue in the top five universities in the nation that provided continuing education and conference programs (Burrin 1988, iv). We can see a steadiness in conference administration, a struggle with Evening Classes, and significant growth in off-campus classes, mediated classes, and professional training, as well as the development of the Maymester summer term overseen by CEA. But Burrin's most significant contributions may have come in his administrative actions.

Building Out an Infrastructure of Policies and Procedures

In a box in the Purdue Archives are several large black three-ring binders full of hundreds of formal procedural and policy memos mostly signed by Frank Burrin. Associate Director Harley Griffith referred to the collection (displayed on his office bookshelf) as his "Bible." The content of those notebooks enumerated how nearly every process in Continuing Education Administration would be handled. Much of that content became so ingrained that it was the "common knowledge" of how things worked in CEA. No other administrator left such a comprehensive legacy of policy and procedure.

Why was such an elaborate system of policy/procedure memos necessary? Why weren't university policies/procedures adequate? Because, from the university perspective, almost every program CEA administered was an anomaly—markedly different from what the university did in its everyday business—that the university's systems and procedures were not equipped to handle. From that perspective, it was the function of CEA to make those anomalies operate reasonably efficiently within the university's administrative systems. Here are some examples of issues that required special attention from CEA administrators:

- How would off-campus students who were not currently seeking a degree be registered for classes? How would they pay their fees? If their fees were paid to CEA, how would those monies be transferred into appropriate university accounts? What university services and privileges would off-campus students have access to?
- If courses were running off the normal university calendar, how would student refunds be calculated and processed?
- If an employer wished to pay the fees for a group of employees, how would the employer be billed and how would payments be processed?
- What university services would conference attendees have access to, such as the recreational gym facilities, the student hospital, or libraries? How would they be recognized as eligible at the point of service?
- How would revenues from Conferences be distributed among the sponsoring academic department, CEA, and the university? The resolution to this question was one of the lasting legacies of Burrin's administration.

Classifying Conferences

In 1977 Burrin implemented a system for classifying conference and short-course activities. A multitude of approaches to a conference classification system were available: by size, by presentational mode (symposium, workshop, roundtable, seminar, etc.), by sponsor (corporate, nonprofit, professional association, etc.), and others. But Burrin chose a different path, one uniquely suited for a university service unit. His classification system was based on who received the benefits of the program, and its types were used to help determine the conference administrative fee for each program. The classification types were as follows:

Type A, University Service: The university or its staff members were the ultimate recipients of benefits accruing from the offering of these programs. No administrative fee was assessed for Type A programs.

Type B, Public Service: The community or general public were the primary or ultimate recipients of the benefits accruing from the offering of these programs. A CEA administrative fee was assessed for Type B programs.

Type C, Individual Service: An individual or the organization represented were the ultimate recipients of the benefits accruing from the offering of these programs. A CEA administrative fee and a university administrative fee were assessed for Type C programs.

Type D, Special Arrangement Meetings: The university, the public, the individual, the organization represented, or all of these may be the ultimate recipients of the benefits accruing from the offering of these programs. Administrative fees for Type D programs varied.

We don't know if this system was conceived by Burrin himself or CEA staff or if it was borrowed from another institutions, but it proved to be very robust at Purdue and has generally continued to be used by Conferences. However, because of costs, Type A programs are now either conducted by the sponsoring unit with no involvement by Conferences or are operated by Conferences as Type B programs. Type C programs were fairly rare and generally involved large organizations and hundreds of participants. Type C conferences created substantial revenues for CEA, campus service units such as the Memorial Union and Residence Halls, and the university itself. Type C program revenues helped to underwrite CEA's costs for pro bono Type A programs.

Other administrative initiatives under Burrin included

- Reviving the dormant University Extension Council as the Continuing Education Council, with representation from each college/school as a coordinating body within the university. Representatives were partially funded by CEA.
- Advocating for and implementing the national standard Continuing Education Unit as a means of providing a valuation of noncredit programs. Burrin also promoted CEUs at the state level through the Indiana Council of Continuing Education, about which more will follow below.
- Supervising the development and implementation of the Purdue Automated Continuing Education Registration System (PACERS) with the cooperation of the university Business Office. PACERS was one of the nation's first fully computerized university registration systems. It remained in use into the 1990s.
- Establishing the Division of Independent Study, which incorporated all of CEA's telecommunications-based programs. By 1979 Independent Study was coordinating Purdue's use of the Indiana Higher Education Telecommunications System (IHETS), thereby establishing CEA as the university's hub for distance learning.

Indiana Council for Continuing Education

Burrin had a strong influence on shaping how continuing education would be conducted at Purdue, but his influence was felt at the state level as well. Burrin and Don Brown were founding members of the Indiana Council for Continuing Education (ICCE), a coordinating body of continuing education units in public and private higher education institutions in Indiana. Burrin served as ICCE's second president. ICCE's objective was to provide a more coordinated approach to higher-learning opportunities for Hoosier adults. This cooperative venture among Indiana's higher education institutions was also a defensive move to stave off regulation of off-campus continuing education activities by the Indiana Commission for Higher Education.

In 1975 Deputy Commissioner Carl Lutz informed the chief academic officers of the state's institutions that the Commission would undertake a "study of existing methods and practices of offering nontraditional programming and . . . explore the advisability of creating a mechanism within the commission to regulate those activities" (Danglade 1990, 6). The study would be carried out by an advisory committee made up of individuals who "represent the academic affairs office of each institution and [are] in position[s] of broader responsibility than an operational continuing education activity on campus" (7). The Commission's plan was not well received by state leaders in continuing education; from their perspective, not only was the Commission contemplating regulating their work, but the Commission was also specifically excluding them from the committee that would make the decision.

In May 1977, the Commission held a meeting with nearly all presidents of the state's higher education institutions. Commissioner Lutz introduced a study of continuing education that would initiate a discussion of "possible models that might be adopted for the coordination of off-campus instruction," and that "after the meeting the Commission staff would be working toward the adoption of a plan for the coordination of off-campus instruction within the state." However, the discussion of the plan among the presidents demonstrated a resistance to any such plan, and the meeting ended without a recommendation for centralizing continuing education. In September, the Commission backed away from such a plan and indicated that "institutions should be given the opportunity to deal cooperatively with any problems involving off-campus credit course offerings" (Danglade 1990, 12).

While ICCE members considered this outcome a success, they also recognized that they needed to cooperate with the Commission and become a source of reliable information about extension activities for the Commission. At this point, Burrin stepped in with a proposal for an Off-Campus Activity Survey: "[Burrin] suggested a questionnaire be distributed at least three times a year requesting information on statewide continuing education activities. Purdue would collect the data received and make a formal detailed report to the membership. Purdue would fund the project, but the report would be issued in the name of ICCE" (12).

The report covered credit and noncredit offerings by institution. It included the activities' contact hours, the number of registrations, the county where offered, types of sites used, and the formats employed. Activities were also classified by the Higher Education General Information System (HEGIS) taxonomy of academic majors and minors. After a review among ICCE members, the report was shared with the Commission, making them fully aware of the institutions' off-campus programs and of the coordination among the institutions. The tri-annual surveys were a major undertaking for CEA, coordinated by Associate Director Harley Griffith. In those days before desktop computers, all the data was received on paper and was transferred into the report by hand. As ICCE institutional memberships grew, the report expanded and became more challenging, but it continued into the early 1990s. In the 1990s and early 2000s off-campus classes were gradually replaced with online courses, extension activities became less geographically based, and traditional off-campus classes and workshops declined. Consequently, the survey became less useful as a representation of the institutions' outreach programs and was eventually dropped. But for two decades Burrin's Off-Campus Activity Survey played an important role in satisfying the Indiana Higher Education Commission's concerns about off-campus offerings by Indiana higher education.

Frank Burrin retired as director of CEA in 1984 and died in 1987. In his thirty-year career in continuing education he did much to formulate how continuing education would be conducted at Purdue. Some of his acumen in policy and programming was undoubtedly due to his being CEA's only director/dean who devoted his entire career to the continuing education enterprise. Associate Provost Donald Brown said Burrin's impact was a tribute to his understanding that "the fundamental reason for the existence of continuing education in a land grant university is to increase access to educational opportunity, which was the primary goal of the Jeffersonian ideal. For that reason, he was a success among his peers, a friend of the people and a valued colleague to those fortunate to work with him" (from Brown's foreword in Burrin 1988, iii). For Burrin's work with ICCE, historian Jim Danglade remembered him as "a giant in the history of continuing education in the state of Indiana" (Danglade 1990, 24).

3

1984–1989

Upon the retirement of CEA director Frank Burrin in 1984, CEA associate director Harley J. Griffith Jr. was appointed interim director of Continuing Education Administration for AY 1984–1985. During that year, a nationwide search was conducted to find a replacement for Burrin. Ultimately, Charles S. Elliott was appointed director of Continuing Education Administration in July of 1985. He had been serving as the director of Continuing Engineering Education in the Purdue School of Engineering.

Elliott had come to Purdue in 1979 as assistant director of Continuing Engineering Education. Before coming to Purdue, he had directed special programs at the College of Engineering at Wayne State University in Detroit, and he worked on the staff of General Motors Institute as director of student activities and services (*Purdue Exponent* 1985).

As director of Continuing Education Administration, Elliott reported to the vice president for academic services, Donald Brown, who oversaw Purdue Libraries, Purdue University Computing Center, WBAA, Center for Instructional Services, and Continuing Education Administration. Brown's office was located with CEA offices on the main floor of Stewart Center, so he was quite engaged with the unit and its director. At roughly the same time that Elliott became director, Brown produced a report entitled "Purdue Extension: Strategies for Renewal" in which he advocated for a broad involvement of the university in the economic vitality of the state, for a commitment to enhancing educational opportunities for a broad swath of citizens, and for the university to play a strong role in support of public schools—their students, teachers, and administrators. A primary vehicle to achieve this vision was the "communiversity," which Brown described as a "cooperative arrangement between Purdue University and a community":

> It is an agreement to provide increased educational opportunity to the citizens of the schools (students, teachers, and administrators) and to the citizens of the community in cooperation with the public schools and other educational institutions in the area. It is a way to bring the resources of the Cooperative Extension Service, Statewide Technology, and the Division of School and Community Programs of Continuing Education to bear upon the educational needs of local communities. It is a way to effectively utilize modern communication systems to deliver Purdue expertise to local communities. (Brown 1985, 47)

Elliott had come to CEA from Continuing Engineering Education, which had been oriented toward technological delivery of high-level professional education to professionals in business and industry at a national and international scale. While his previous experience probably had not prepared him for the concept of the "communiversity," he organized CEA to help advance it. Upon being appointed CEA director, Elliott reorganized the office into four divisions (down from the previous nine divisions):

- Administrative services (led by Harley Griffith)
- Media-based programs (led by Shirley Davis)
- School and community programs (led by Shirley Smith)
- Professional programs (led by Chuck Elliott)—a new division that consisted of representatives from the different schools that offered continuing education programs. The representatives reported to their respective school deans. The unit was designed to promote communication and cooperation across the campus.

In 1986 Elliott created the position of communications coordinator, reporting directly to him. The position was intended to improve Continuing Education's communication with the clients and prospective clients on campus and to enhance communication with the communities CEA served. Michael Eddy was hired for the position. In 1988 the position of Coordinator for School Programs was added to School and Community Programs to help build out the education support aspect of the "communiversity." Deborah Ruckman was hired for the position.

Elliott was a believer in "management by objectives," and he insisted that his staff follow this same philosophy. Consequently, he initiated a more decentralized approach to management than had been used in the past, with each director being responsible for attaining agreed-upon objectives (Schmitt 1985).

With respect to programming, CEA was engaged in supporting course offerings on campus and off campus through traditional classroom instruction and technology-driven means. Some continuing education courses and programs were delivered as correspondence courses, but others used the most advanced technology of that day, broadcast via satellite. Purdue was one of eighteen universities offering this type of delivery through National Technological University (NTU) in the fall of 1985. Lectures were bounced off the G-Star satellite from member institutions' home campuses or were forwarded to NTU on videotape for satellite transmission (Carlson 1985, 31). This allowed engineers and computer technicians, assembled in distant company/organization classrooms, to watch the lectures on television, take notes, and question the professors by telephone or "computer mail."

ON-CAMPUS PROGRAMS

On campus, CEA had sole authority to schedule undergraduate classes after 5 p.m. Originally, evening classes were intended primarily for community members, and on-campus students could only enroll in them by special permission. As noted earlier, by the 1980s, demand within the community had fallen off and evening classes had been opened to Purdue campus students. By 1989, evening class enrollments were split evenly between campus students and nontraditional students. As more campus students enrolled in evening classes, the financial situation for evening classes became more precarious, because CEA recovered no tuition from full-time students. Between 1986 and 1989, CEA offered an average of 125 evening classes per year; enrollments averaged 3,303.

Another area of on-campus credit programming was the Maymester program of four-week, intensive credit courses. Maymester grew out of a desire for such courses to be made available as expressed by Purdue Student Government. In 1981 Student Government conducted a survey of students concerning their interest in intersession courses and what courses would be useful to them. The survey became the basis for CEA's course offerings in 1982. CEA had authorization to offer summer intensive courses but had done so only sparingly. Because of the intense nature of the courses, students were allowed to enroll in only one course per Maymester term. Maymester proved a very popular program, growing its enrollments an average of 19 percent in its first seven years. The program was initially managed by Don Rons and followed by John Almon in 1986, both of CEA's Special Classes division. By the end of Elliott's tenure in 1989, Maymester offered forty courses with 1,056 enrollments.

Off-Campus Courses

Away from campus, CEA was offering Purdue credit courses in about forty communities throughout Indiana. During Elliott's administration (1986–1989), an average of thirty-seven courses with 480 enrollments were offered in the state's northern region, while the southwest region averaged forty-two classes with 714 enrollments. Most of these classes were offered at local high schools during evening hours to accommodate working adults. CEA regional managers typically drove to sites to register students and collect course fees. In some cases, CEA managers sold students the texts they would need for their courses. Money handling was a concern, and bonded CEA Business Office personnel generally accompanied the regional managers to off-campus registrations.

Purdue Continuing Education Administration also offered many courses through the Indiana Higher Education Telecommunications System (IHETS) satellite network. The IHETS system featured two-way audio and one-way video to support teacher and learner interaction. The courses/programs were received in plants and at public access sites (Bonhomme 1988).

In the late 1980s the infrastructure for electronic distribution of courses was closed-circuit television or satellite transmission, both requiring special receiving equipment. Distance learning offered through IHETS was oriented to mid-career professionals and available only at authorized sites such as businesses or hospitals. Consequently, a demand existed for in-person classes of a more general nature. This demand was especially acute in southeast Indiana, which was distant from any main or regional university campus. The population of the region was primarily rural and was considered not sufficiently dense enough to sustain a full regional campus.

The challenges of offering in-person classes in a thinly populated region were numerous. Finding the critical mass of students for a class offering to be financially feasible was difficult. Often students would have to drive significant distances to attend classes. Finding local instructors sufficiently qualified to teach college-level courses was difficult. As students advanced through their curriculum and their courses became more specialized, identifying instructors and generating a critical mass of students for higher-level classes became increasingly difficult.

The College of Technology's Statewide Technology program was enjoying success with a network of eight centers throughout the state that offered a limited set of Purdue associate degree programs aligned with identifiable needs in the area. Local postsecondary institutions delivered general education courses for Statewide Technology degree programs, while Statewide Technology delivered the technically oriented courses.

Southeast Extension Center

Don Brown was looking for a pilot site for his "communiversity" concept: "Southeast Indiana, centered on the Versailles area, would be an excellent location to develop the Communiversity idea" (Brown 1985, 50). He noted that Purdue had been offering courses in Versailles for more than twenty years, and those courses were enrolling about 1,600 students annually. Statewide Technology was planning to offer a degree program there. And Purdue had strong relations with an educational planning group in the area. In addition, there was vocal demand for more higher-education programming in the region from business leaders, especially Hillenbrand Industries in Batesville. Hillenbrand's founder and president had served on Purdue's Board of Trustees; a few years later a new residence hall on campus would be named for the Hillenbrand family.

In 1986 Brown proposed to consolidate Purdue's Southeast Indiana course offerings around the Purdue University Southeastern Extension Center based in Versailles. The center would host Statewide Technology's offering of its associate degree in supervision and would provide general education courses for degree-seeking students and southeast Indiana communities at large. This arrangement followed the model that had been successful for Statewide Technology in other locales around the state. Terry Sargent, a history teacher in Lakeland and Jennings county schools, was hired to direct the center, which became a unit of CEA's School and Community Programs division.

The Versailles center quickly became a robust enterprise. By 1988 Versailles had the highest enrollments of any of the eight Statewide Technology sites. During Elliott's tenure the Southeast Extension Center offered about one hundred course sections per year, and enrollments rose from about 1,000 to 1,400. Classes were offered in high schools off-hours in ten southeast Indiana counties in Sellersburg, Milan, Batesville, Lawrenceburg, and other towns.

Growth in Conferences

Back on campus the conference business was flourishing. Director of Conferences Gary Lee noted Purdue's conference success as follows: "The volume of conference activity at Purdue has established it as one of the four largest university conference centers in the United States, if not the world" (CEA Annual Report, 1988–89, 11). From 1986 through 1989, conference business grew steadily:

Years	Programs	Attendees
1986–87	391	83,694
1987–88	451	91,694
1988–89	437	96,139

All Purdue conferences were sponsored by Purdue academic units. In Elliott's final year of 1989, Continuing Education Administration was the most active conference sponsor with ninety-seven programs and 45,617 attendees, which comprised nearly a quarter of the programs and nearly half of the attendees. In Burrin's classification system, many were Type A programs, which CEA administered at no charge. Others were meetings of external organizations that desired to meet on campus, which were classified as Type C and hence were revenue sources for CEA. The second largest sponsor of Conferences was the College of Agriculture with 134 programs and 16,900 attendees. A staff of seven coordinators in CEA's Conference Division supported these programs. In 1988 coordinator Kathy Hyman assumed a new half-time role as business and industry coordinator with the goal of expanding CEA's engagement with Indiana's private sector. This initiative would become more active under the next director.

In 1989 Elliott announced that he was leaving Purdue to assume a new position at Arizona State University.

4

1989–1998

In June 1989 Vice President Don Brown announced that Richard O. Forsythe would serve as acting director of the Continuing Education Administration in addition to his role as director of the Division of Instructional Services. Forsythe was named CEA's permanent director in 1991 and continued in that position through 1998. On assuming the directorship on a permanent basis, Forsythe had the name Continuing Education Administration shortened to Continuing Education (CE), and the Division of Instructional Services became the Center for Instructional Services (CIS).

Brown brought Forsythe into Continuing Education not because Forsythe had a particular background in the field but because Brown knew him to be an able administrator. Forsythe had taken on management of several administrative units under Brown's purview and consolidated them into the Division of Instructional Services. (Forsythe once calculated that his management had saved the university four million dollars and cited the figure often.) He was focused on administering programs in an efficient and transparent manner and making CE maximally valuable to the university. This meant that he looked hard at areas and programs that were not holding their own financially and that he was very straightforward about financial matters and explicit about how the university, academic units, and faculty members benefitted financially from continuing education programs. He looked for ways to combine the resources of CE and CIS to create greater efficiencies and to offer a broader range of services. Forsythe described his new dual role in the 1989–90 annual report as follows: "This joint administrative structure created opportunities to share talent and resources, eliminate redundancies, and standardize procedures." In an addendum to his 1990–91 annual report, he noted an additional goal of "increased departmental emphasis on the bottom line."

Don Brown's "communiversity" approach was still very much in play, but Forsythe, with Brown's blessing, was determined to demonstrate how the university benefitted from continuing education initiatives. That approach had efficacy as the university entered a period of tight resources and especially as Brown stepped down from his vice presidency in 1993. At that juncture CE/CIS moved under the purview of Executive Vice President for Academic Affairs Robert Ringel, with Forsythe reporting directly to Assistant Executive Vice President George Van Scoyoc. With this perspective, Forsythe's initiatives were administratively focused, including the Operational Processes Group, the Joint Operations Conferences Marketing Committee, and the Communications Group. Like Frank Burrin, Forsythe also focused on enhancing CE's infrastructure of policies and procedures to deliver the kinds of programs the university desired and operate them in compliance with the university's policy and procedures.

The following CE units reported to Forsythe as director:

- Conferences—Associate Director, Gary Lee
- Administrative Services—Associate Director, Harley Griffith
    - Distance and Media-Based Education Programs—Manager, Jenny Towler
    - Restaurant, Hotel, and Institutional Management Institute—Manager, Lee Kruel
    - Insurance Marketing Institute—Manager, Eugene Broecker
    - Self-Directed Learning—Manager, Sueann Smith
- School and Community Programs—Associate Director, Shirley Smith
    - Special Classes and Lafayette Extension Region—Manager, John Almon
    - Economic Education Programs—Manager, Pete Harrington
    - Gifted Education Programs—Coordinator, Mary Gardner
    - Educational Travel Programs—Manager, Joann Chaney
    - Northern and Southwestern Extension Region—Manager, Jim Wagner
    - Southeastern Extension Region—Coordinator, Terry Sargent
- Data Systems—Manager, Gary Wright
- Information Services—Manager, Mike Eddy
- CE Business Office—Business Administrator, Judy Casey

These units together served more than one hundred thirty thousand participants annually. The Conference Division, alone, supported over 350 programs and attracted over sixty thousand attendees to the West Lafayette campus in 1990. This made it one of the largest and most well-respected university conference centers in the country.

Purdue's president, Steven C. Beering, said in 1990 that he was surprised at the large number of people enrolled in Continuing Education courses in 1988–89 (137,281 according to CE's annual report). Beering went on to say: "The variety of Continuing Education programs is simply staggering. They range from regular credit courses to weekly hours in things like auto repair or cooking taken for pure enjoyment. Engineers, pharmacists, teachers and other professionals use them to update their skills. This is one of the important, but often unnoticed, ways Purdue University enhances our state's economy and quality of life" (Black 1990, 4).

CE/CIS Synergies

Forsythe was quick to recognize areas of synergy between the conjoined Continuing Education and Center for Instructional Services. CE had hired Charlie Russell to support its growing fleet of PCs and its desktop publishing operation. CIS had a Data Services unit directed by Gary Wright that supported the CAFETERIA course/instructor evaluation system, scheduling databases for classroom services, and network connections to university systems. In Forsythe's first year, Data Services became a shared unit, with Russell moving into it. The new unit was charged with developing systems and programs for CE and coordinating computer purchases. They planned a local area network that would link CE and CIS to the campus fiber network, the university's Administrative Data Processing Center (ADPC), and the Purdue University Computing Center (PUCC). Data Systems also began developing a new event registration system to replace the Purdue Automated Continuing Education Registration System (PACERS) that had been developed in the 1970s. They also made it possible for the Southeast Extension Center to access West Lafayette registration files. In his 1989–90 annual report to Brown, Forsythe noted that "by relying on in-house computer expertise, we will be able to develop our next generation of computer services for less than half the price of purchasing such services from ADPC [Purdue's Administrative Data Processing Center]."

A second joint CE/CIS unit was established to coordinate the departments' promotional activities, exercise quality control over marketing materials, oversee desktop publishing, and help develop marketing programs. The Marketing Division, managed by Mike Eddy, produced newsletters for CE, CIS, and WBAA, as well as marketing materials for CE programs and CIS services. The unit was also charged with mounting a nationwide marketing effort to attract new conference business. Shortly after Forsythe submitted his first annual report, Brown informed him that universities don't do "marketing," and the joint unit was rechristened Information Services.

Reviewing Operational Processes

Forsythe established the Operational Processes Group (OPG) to methodically review CE's business processes and find ways to improve them with respect to customer service and compliance with university business standards. (He had reluctantly abandoned his first name for the group—Process Improvement Group or PIG.) Longtime CE associate director Harley Griffith called the initiative "Dick Forsythe's orientation to Continuing Education," but more was behind it than that. In the 1989–90 annual report, Forsythe wrote that "in response to University concern about reimbursement [of faculty] for continuing education activities," he had put in place a new process that ensured that permission had been granted on the academic side for the faculty to be paid overload. He also noted that he was reviewing all CE activity budgets and letters of agreement. In the next year, he reported that "because of system-wide attention to overload," CE had participated in the rewriting of Executive Memorandum C-18, which simplified overload payments but also reduced the level of overload faculty could earn. He also noted that the Dean's Council conducted a review of CE in April. He also reported new procedures with the Graduate School to ensure that all instructors in the 590 CE-administered graduate courses were members of the graduate faculty. Clearly, there were a variety of "concerns" and considerable scrutiny about CE operations at the university level with respect to finances, authorization, and business processes. No doubt Brown's choice of the administratively adept Forsythe had much to do with these "concerns." OPG gave Forsythe a structure through which to address these matters systematically.

OPG met every other week, and afternoon meetings were scheduled for two hours but often ran longer. Attendees included everyone with administrative responsibility in CE, managers of Information Services and Data Service, administrators from the Business Office, and others. Usually two or three issues were in process at any given time. Issues were discussed, and appropriate documents were drafted, submitted to the group for discussion, and revised until all parties were satisfied. Eddy and Forsythe would do as many as ten iterations of documents. Forsythe was focused, patient, and eager to get a handle on all the intricate "nuts and bolts" of CE processes. Accomplishments of the OPG initiative included:

- One-working-day turnaround of registrations
- Acceptance of credit cards as payments for fees (long before the university as a whole accepted credit cards)
- A customizable electronic Letter of Agreement that specified what services would be delivered accompanied by an information sheet specifying all the university policies and procedures the program would be subject to
- Annual closings of program accounts to ensure financial transparency and appropriate distribution of funds
- Procedures for compliance with the new federal law, the Americans with Disabilities Act

Many of these processes and documents remained in place for decades, probably because of the care and attention to detail that went into their formulation.

Communiversity Programs

In terms of programming, elements of Brown's "communiversity" remained strong. Community-oriented evening classes remained robust with about 120 courses and averaging over 2,930 enrollments annually. These classes were financially challenged, however, as full-time Purdue students came to dominate the enrollments. CE received no revenues for students paying full-time fees; all operating costs had to be covered by part-time community students. Noncredit community courses declined, perhaps due to increased competition in this space from Ivy Tech, the Greater Lafayette Art Museum, and local churches. In Forsythe's first three years the number of campus-based noncredit courses dropped 60 percent. In that period off-campus credit courses held their own, with over 70 percent of extension classes and enrollments being delivered through the Southeastern Extension Center in Versailles.

A new "communiversity" initiative arose in 1992 as Greater Lafayette community members began discussions with the Elderhostel Institute to offer noncredit enrichment courses for Greater Lafayette seniors. The community group wanted to affiliate themselves with Elderhostel Institute but needed a university sponsor—hence Purdue's involvement. Mary Gardner, who had been coordinating gifted education programs for School and Community Programs, was designated as Purdue's representative to what would become known as the Wabash Area Life-long Learning Association (WALLA). The citizen's group defined the curriculum for its fall and spring offerings; CE served as the financial agent, handled logistics, and assisted with securing instructors as needed. Gardner continued to work with WALLA for three decades as it grew into a valued community resource.

The association with Elderhostel Institute inspired Gardner to try offering a summer Elderhostel program open to seniors around the country. The initial program was a choral singing workshop offered in conjunction with the Purdue Varsity Glee Club. That proved very popular, so Gardner expanded to a second offering based on Purdue research initiatives, featuring Purdue investigators presenting their research in plain language to attendees. Both Elderhostels continued for more than a decade, drawing senior participants from across the country.

Another "communiversity" program was study tours, which Forsythe had become intrigued with as a vehicle to enrich the education of campus students and the continuing education of area residents. The tours would range from a week to a month in duration, would be led by Purdue faculty with relevant expertise, and would be supported by on-site tour providers to coordinate logistics. The instructors could make the tours available for credit with additional academic components. In 1989 the initial tours were coordinated by Jim Wagner, who handled CE's Northern Extension region. In 1991 study tours became the responsibility of Joann Chaney, who had conducted successful art/architecture tours of Rome. Study tours continued to be offered throughout Forsythe's tenure to such destinations as England, France, Greece, Egypt, the Galapagos, and many others. Typically, about ten programs were offered a year, nearly all in summer, with about 100 to 150 total participants.

However gratifying for attendees, study tours were challenging to administer. Their logistics were very complicated, relatively few people could be accommodated on any given trip, and the success of programs to new destinations was unpredictable. Nearly all of the details of a program had to be worked out before a tour could be marketed, so the investment in a program that didn't make the schedule was almost as high as in one that did. Consequently, the study tours program always operated at the edge of fiscal viability. When Forsythe stepped down as director in 1999, CE's study tours were subsumed into the university's International Programs office; Chaney retired shortly thereafter.

One milestone "communiversity" program ceased in the early 1990s. In negotiations with Indiana University president Myles Brand, Purdue president Steven Beering arranged that administration of the Southeast Extension Center in Versailles, perhaps the cornerstone of Don Brown's "communiversity" project, would be turned over to Indiana University. The rationale presented was that the center was within IU's area of service, loosely defined as south of Indianapolis. Other machinations may have been in play as well. The center had been struggling financially, but the agreement between the presidents came as a surprise to CE administrators.

Maymester

Maymester, the intersession intensive courses CE administered for the campus, grew steadily in Forsythe's first three years. In 1992–93 Maymester saw a 53 percent growth in classes (from 49 to 75) and 48 percent growth in enrollments (from 1,371 to 2,039). This development was enough to convince Executive Vice President for Academic Affairs Robert Ringel to incorporate Maymester into the regular university schedule. Because CE was capturing the majority of fee revenues from Maymester courses, this migration was a significant blow—an estimated loss of $250,000 in operating funds, resulting in some layoffs and operational cutbacks. Fortunately, the Reading Recovery program of credit courses for early-grade elementary school teachers grew sufficiently to cover that financial loss within three years. A primary reason for Maymester's success was that CE's administrator, John Almon, based offerings on the needs of students as determined by surveys of students running in the *Purdue Exponent* in early offerings. CE administrators were proud to have developed a program that would become an important element in Purdue's academic offerings and a genuine aid to students' being able to complete their studies in a timely manner.

Marketing Conferences

In considering how Purdue could expand its conference business, Forsythe and Conferences associate director Gary Lee concluded that "megaconferences" were the opportunity to pursue. Megaconferences were meetings of over one thousand attendees and generally were offered in conjunction with external organizations, making CE the sponsoring academic unit. Purdue's primary advantage in this market was its vast residence hall system, which was greatly underutilized in the summer months, and Stewart Center's dedicated conference space. Also, the Elliott Hall of Music was a unique venue for special programs, able to seat six thousand people comfortably with excellent acoustics and professional-quality staging. Also, attendees generally felt safe and secure on the Purdue campus. Among the challenges of megaconferences were a very short window of summer availability (about eight weeks), largely non-air-conditioned housing facilities, and a lack of amenities and attractions in Greater Lafayette. The competition for megaconferences was very high, not just from other universities but also convention facilities in big-city downtowns. Conferences had already won a contract with Presbyterian Youth Triennium, which brought over four thousand high schoolers to campus every third year.

Because residence halls and the Purdue Memorial Union benefited from megaconferences, Forsythe coordinated in 1991 with Housing and Food Services vice president Ron Fruitt to create a joint conferences marketing group with a line of funding from HFS and CE. The partnership continued after Fruitt retired in 1996 and was replaced by John Sautter. Chaired by Mike Eddy, the Joint Operations Marketing Committee consisted of a representative from Residence Hall Administration, Sue Graham; from the Union, Bob Mindrum; from the Union Club Hotel, Jerry Day; from CIS, Bonnie Eddy; from Hall of Music, Steve Hall; and from Conferences Gary Lee and Kathy Hyman. It also included representatives of the Greater Lafayette Convention and Visitors' Bureau, Jo Wade and Elaine McVay. The marketing group began to promote Purdue's conference capabilities by advertising in trade publications of the meeting industry and attending some trade shows, most consistently the Religious Conference Managers' Association meeting. The group worked with the CIS media producer Ed Dunn on a video presentation, "The Purdue Conference Complex," which won the 1993 national Bronze award for video presentation from the University Continuing Education Association (UCEA). Later the group worked with the Office of Publications to produce the "Simply Success" mixed media campaign package, which was awarded the UCEA's 1997 Gold Mixed Media Campaign Award. All told, Purdue conference marketing materials won six UCEA national and regional marketing awards. In the summer of 1994, the group's efforts resulted in three megaconferences: Faith Works, a religious conference of about four thousand attendees; the National Order of the Arrow, a scouting program of about seven thousand; and Accelerated Christian Education with about three thousand attendees.

In 1998 the committee worked with Sam Florance of the Krannert School of Management to develop a business plan for Purdue conferences. The purpose of the plan was to develop a more strategic approach to marketing Purdue conference services. The study showed that in its first five years the committee's marketing efforts had produced programs that generated $6,398,794 in gross revenues; expenses for that marketing had totaled only 2 percent of that amount, far below the benchmark 10 percent. The study showed that total conference revenues were subject to significant swings due to the presence or absence of megaconferences. The study also demonstrated that nearly half of the marketing-generated revenues went to residence halls. So the recommended strategy was to continue to pursue megaconferences but to also pursue smaller conferences that could help even out the revenue flow. The plan proposed to increase marketing staff by .75 FTE and to increase funding for marketing activities by $10,000. Forsythe and Sautter approved the proposal. In the two years that followed, the committee's efforts brought twenty-seven conferences to Purdue.

Richard Forsythe stepped down as CE director at the end of 1998. After a decade of work, he had made CE into a more professionally run operation, with transparency in finances. He returned to directing CIS. In 2002 he took advantage of Purdue Voluntary Early Partial Retirement and with reduced work hours he worked on special projects with Vice President for Engagement Don Gentry and filled in as the director of Conferences for a year upon Gary Lee's retirement. Forsythe retired fully in 2007 after fifty years of service to the university.

5

1999–2002

IN JANUARY 1999 PHILIP H. SWAIN WAS APPOINTED assistant executive vice president for academic affairs and director of the newly formulated Office for Instructional Excellence and Lifelong Learning (OIELL), which consisted of the Center for Lifelong Learning (formerly Continuing Education), the Center for Instructional Excellence (formerly the Division of Instructional Services within Center for Instructional Services (CIS)), and the Division of Instructional Services (formerly CIS). In 2001 Swain's OIELL title was changed from director to dean; he was the first continuing education administrator to be a dean since Charles Lawshe retired in 1974.

Immediately prior to assuming his CE position, Swain had directed Purdue's Office of Distance Learning, beginning in April 1997. The office was newly created for Swain and was not continued after he moved to OIELL. As director of Distance Learning he initiated the first Purdue distance learning strategic plan, which involved a wide range of people from many administrative offices and academic departments serving on a Distance Learning Advisory Board. The plan absorbed the entire period of his tenure in Distance Learning and was completed and distributed after Swain assumed his OIELL position. Swain also directed Continuing Engineering Education (CEE) from 1986 through 1997. Like Chuck Elliott, Swain had deep experience with the delivery of advanced higher education through technology in CEE. During the latter part of Swain's tenure as CEE director and through his tenure as director of Distance Learning, Swain chaired the working group for the Indiana Partnership for Higher Education (IPSE), which resulted in the Indiana College Network (ICN), which is discussed below. With Swain's bona fides in distance learning, his selection to head OIELL sent a clear signal that the university intended to advance distance learning at Purdue.

That implied mandate undergirds Swain's description of his new position in a Purdue news release:

The motivation for this restructuring is rooted in the dramatic changes taking place across the higher education landscape, especially those related to changing demographics and the impact of technology in academe. The new organization will enhance Purdue's ability to address the needs of students of all ages and to support an increasingly technology-oriented work force for which lifelong learning is inescapable. It, also, will assist the faculty in the development and adoption of innovative uses of technology to make teaching and learning more effective and to make the considerable educational resources of Purdue more accessible to the citizens of our state and nation. (Purdue News Service, 1999)

All the goals noted by Swain above would be accomplished through the technological advances in distance learning. This turn to distance learning would become more pronounced in the first decades of the twenty-first century. At Purdue, "continuing education" would become effectively synonymous with "distance education."

Indiana Partnership for Higher Education/Indiana College Network

Swain's greatest contribution to distance learning at Purdue, and throughout Indiana, was his deep involvement with shaping the Indiana Partnership for Higher Education and its course delivery entity, the Indiana College Network. The parent organization was the Indiana Higher Education Telecommunication System (IHETS), formed with support from the Commission for Higher Education. IHETS was established by the 1967 Indiana Higher Education Telecommunications Act. The act authorized the state universities to "jointly arrange . . . for the use of a multipurpose, multimedia, closed-circuit, statewide telecommunications system . . . to interconnect the campuses of the universities and centers of medical education and service." Throughout the 1970s and 1980s, primary users of the IHETS system were Purdue Cooperative Extension Service, Purdue Continuing Engineering Education, and the Medical Education Network, in which Purdue participated with other Indiana institutions. In the late 1980s IHETS, with the support of the Indiana Commission for Higher Education, began to explore how its system might be used to provide broader access to formal higher education courses and programs.

In August 1992 the IHETS Board of Directors launched the Indiana Partnership for Statewide Education (IPSE) to "assure statewide access to postsecondary education through active collaboration among member institutions." Swain was appointed as the chair of the IPSE working group and was very active in that role, both in working to shape the Partnership and in engaging Purdue administrators and faculty to join in the implementation process. That engagement was not automatically forthcoming.

When Swain, as IPSE chair, wrote to Don Brown requesting Brown's help in identifying individuals who should attend IPSE's first All Partners Conference in December, 1992, Brown was inspired to write to Executive Vice President Robert Ringel as follows:

> The activities of Phil Swain are interesting. It seems to me that he is in the process of trying to invent something which, in the absence of a better title, we might call the Continuing Education Administration.
>
> As you know, CEA has been responsible for operating off-campus credit courses for the academic deans. We have also been responsible for so-called "distance education" courses. We have in place all the mechanisms for admission, registration, collecting tuition and fees, paying direct instruction costs, and distributing funds to relevant University departments. . . . Doesn't it seem a bit odd to have Phil Swain reinventing all those things under the auspices of the "Partnership of [sic] Statewide Education"? (Don Brown memo to Robert Ringel and Richard Grace, November 23, 1992)

Despite Brown's skepticism, Swain persisted and obtained the participation of Rich Wells (bursar), Bill Murray (admissions), Barbara Doster (academic advising), Tom Gunderson/Camilla Lawson (registrar), as well as many other administrators and faculty members. Swain and these others remained vitally engaged in a two-year endeavor to develop a working entity that would make distance learning courses from all twenty-six IPSE member institutions available to all students at those institutions and to independent learners.

The process that evolved would require students wishing to take a course from another institution to register for an equivalent course at their home institution and to be enrolled in a section at their home institution in which the instruction would be provided by the offering IPSE partner institution. Students would pay tuition and fees for the course to their home institution. At the semester's end the bursar would distribute 90 percent of the tuition to the partner institution providing the instruction. By keeping students enrolled only at their home institution, their Financial Aid could be applied to IPSE courses. This process had many moving parts and required a great deal of administrative work behind the scenes, but it worked well to provide Indiana students with access to courses they needed.

The entity that emerged to deliver these services across the state came to be known as the Indiana College Network (ICN). The branding and the accompanying marketing materials were developed by the IPSE Marketing Committee, on which CE's Michael Eddy served for two years. The Marketing Committee worked in cooperation with an Indianapolis marketing firm.

ICN launched in July 1994. It was built upon a searchable database of course listings from IPSE member institutions and an online preregistration system by which the student's home institution and the host institution became aware of the student's interest and initiated the registration and financial processes. IPSE and ICN were rather unique in their coordination of distance learning on a statewide basis and were much admired throughout the country. Phil Swain played a critical role in their development. IPSE/ICN played an important role in the tenure of two CE deans who succeeded Swain.

Extended University

The OIELL units Swain oversaw and their leadership were as follows:

- Center for Lifelong Learning—Philip Swain, director
  - Extended University—Michael Eddy, director
  - Distributed Learning Services—Joetta Burrous, director
- Center for Instructional Excellence— James Lehman, interim director and Marne Helgesen, director
- Division of Instructional Services—Richard Forsythe, director
- Data Systems—Gary Wright, director

Extended University was essentially the former Continuing Education minus the Conference division, which resided in Instructional Services under Forsythe. Extended University's focus was the delivery of educational programs. Distributed Learning Services existed to build up the campus infrastructure for distance learning.

Extended University carried forward with Continuing Education's program portfolio. Most of that portfolio was classroom based, not distance learning. With the loss of the Southeast Extension Center in Versailles, the delivery of courses at off-campus locations had substantially declined; in 1999–2000 only twenty off-campus classes were offered with a total of 657 registrants. These courses were being gradually replaced by online courses delivered at learning centers by IPSE partners through ICN. Evening Classes, Study Tours, and WALLA/Elderhostel programs for seniors continued.

The distance learning portfolio was substantial, however. In 1999–2000, CLL reported that it assisted in the administration of 125 distance learning programs in which 9,122 learners participated. These included the new veterinary technology distance learning associate degree program (the university's first undergraduate degree to be delivered entirely online), the School of Technology Weekend Master's Degree, Krannert's Executive Master's Degree, the Executive Master of Business Administration in Food and Agribusiness, the International Master's in Management, the Nontraditional Doctor of Pharmacy, and multiple master's degrees in engineering offered through Continuing Engineering Education. Correspondence courses were still an important element in distance learning; in 1999–2000, CLL supported thirteen correspondence courses, largely noncredit, in which 7,017 working professionals enhanced their credentials. The largest such courses were a pest management course offered through the Entomology Department that prepared technicians for certification exams in most states, and a course in sterile processing in health care offered with the International Association of Healthcare Central Service Materiel Management in conjunction with their certification program.

Distributed Learning Services

Distributed Learning Services was engaged in building an infrastructure for distance learning at Purdue. DLS developed a policy framework for distance learning courses and programs to clarify administrative responsibility. This framework included distance learning fees for in-state and out-of-state students. CLL administrators were concerned about Purdue distance learning courses being competitively priced in the national market, and some institutions were pricing their distance learning courses at their in-state rates for all students. However, the solution that was arrived at was a compromise: in-state students would pay the Board of Trustees–approved hourly rate (with no additional distance learning fee) and out-of-state students would pay 150 percent of the in-state fee, which was substantially less than normal out-of-state fees. Significant as these fees were, in practice they were little used. Full-time Purdue students paid their fees in a block once they were registered for nine or more credit hours. Distance learning degree programs could set market-based fees through CLL by annually making a rate request to the Treasurer's Office, so the default 150 percent fee rarely came into play.

In support of the Cooperative Extension Service and Indiana Higher Education Telecommunication System (IHETS) initiative to establish learning centers in communities throughout the state, Distributed Learning Services partnered with those agencies to develop and offer Creating Learning Communities, a one-day conference attended by over four hundred community educators and academics. On campus, DLS helped coordinate Teaching at a Distance Primer workshops as well as teleconferences on distance learning; these programs were attended by over two hundred faculty members. DLS also coordinated the new distance learning awards that were sponsored by the president and the executive vice president for academic affairs. These awards became part of the annual university awards convocation and helped build campus awareness of distance learning.

Growth in Distance Learning

As infrastructure around distance learning began to take shape, student interest in distance learning was becoming evident. In previous years only about ten Purdue students had participated in distance learning courses offered by other Indiana colleges and universities through the Indiana College Network. In 2000–2001 that number had grown to one hundred , and in the next decade it would grow to more than 4,000.

Other OIELL units were helpful collaborators in CLL's efforts to advance distance learning. The Center for Instructional Excellence was responsible for providing development and deployment of innovative approaches to teaching and learning, including those incorporating emerging technologies. While CIE was not addressing distance learning in its instructional workshops, it did assist CLL in developing a Distance Learning Checklist to help faculty design distance learning courses consistent with North Central Accrediting Association standards. After a national search, Marne Helgesen from the University of Illinois became CIE's first director in October 2000.

The Division of Instructional Services (DIS) provided instructional support including audiovisual, photographics, art, media production, and broadcast services, all of which were available to distance learning instructors. DIS supported the implementation of new teaching technologies in the classroom especially through establishing the Multimedia Instructional Development Center (MIDC) in 1997 and hiring John Campbell as its first director. In the transition to OIELL, MIDC migrated to administration of the Computing Center. In 1999–2000, DIS established a portable videoconferencing capability so that video conferencing could be conducted from any campus classroom. In 2000–01, DIS distributed twenty-six credit courses and ninety-five noncredit courses through its satellite services, and it initiated an orientation program for first-time distance instructors. DIS also initiated video streaming services, streaming 144 hours of instruction on the Internet.

In 2000–01, the Data Systems Group partnered with the Registrar's Office to create a new database to "authenticate" OIELL part-time and distance learning students to make Library and Computing Center services available to them. Data Systems developed and launched the Purdue Events Tracking System (PETS), which allowed OIELL program coordinators to monitor and modify data on scheduled campus programs. Data Systems also constructed custom registration databases for the mega-conferences United Methodist Men and Presbyterian Youth Triennium, with a combined eleven thousand participants.

During 1999–2000, the Conference Division administered 816 Purdue conferences which were attended by 85,098 participants. In 2000–2001, 691 conferences were conducted with 70,012 attendees from Indiana, states across the nation, and countries throughout the world. Longtime Conferences director Gary Lee retired in 1999. Former director Richard Forsythe served as interim director while a nationwide search was conducted for Lee's replacement. Paul Horngren, who directed the conference operation of the University of Wisconsin–Oshkosh, was hired as the new director of Conferences.

Phil Swain announced his retirement in August 2002. His tenure was relatively brief, but it set a course for Continuing Education in distance learning that would endure for the next two decades. The structure he established for OIELL was one that allowed its units to continue to perform their unique functions but to also help build the university's capacity to develop and deliver distance learning. Though Swain's commitment to distance learning meant Conferences received relatively little of his attention, the unit flourished under Forsythe in OIELL's Division of Instructional Services.

6

2002–2011

Upon the departure of Philip Swain in May of 2002, Mark A. Pagano was named interim dean. After receiving his doctorate in engineering science from Southern Illinois University, Carbondale, Pagano joined Purdue in 1992 as a faculty member in the mechanical engineering technology department. He later was named head of the department and served as both assistant and then associate dean of the college.

Like other changes in leadership, Pagano's appointment included a charge to restructure the department. The unit was renamed the Office of Continuing Education and Conferences (OCEC) at that time, largely for purposes of clarity. Pagano reported to Don Gentry, Purdue vice provost for engagement, and formerly dean of the School of Technology. Gentry's new position had just been established in August 2001 to reflect the Jischke administration's emphasis on outreach to the state of Indiana. Gentry's Office of Engagement incorporated several outreach-oriented units, such as the Technical Assistance Program. With regard to OCEC, Gentry said "This new structure positions the various continuing education opportunities at Purdue in a way that better serves the people that use them. . . . We anticipate that the office will continue to serve in the role of advocate for part-time and nontraditional students who typically live off campus" (Purdue News Service, 2002).

The new Office of Continuing Education and Conferences oversaw all the activities previously associated with the Center for Lifelong Learning, except for educational travel programs which migrated to the Office of the Dean of International Programs. The new office reincorporated the Conference Division, which had been located within the Division of Instructional Services during Swain's tenure.

Paul Horngren became the new director of Conferences, reporting directly to Pagano. Horngren came to Purdue from the University of Wisconsin–Oshkosh, where he had been the director of the Gruenhagen Conference Center for six years. Horngren chaired a new initiative called Purdue Conferences Coordinating Council. This council included the directors of:

- Purdue Memorial Union—Robert Mindrum
- The Elliott Hall of Music—Stephen Hall
- The Office of Business Managers—Marilyn Kantz
- The University Calendar Office—Jennifer Ricksey
- The Division of Recreational Sports—Larry Preo
- The Greater Lafayette Convention and Visitors Bureau—Jo Wade

Reorganizing

Many units that had been part of OIELL did not continue in the new Office for Continuing Education and Conferences. The Center for Instructional Excellence became a free-standing unit under the Provost's Office. The Division of Instructional Services was essentially absorbed into the Office of the Vice President for Information Technology. The reassigned units included instructional technology, audiovisual support, instructional data processing and data systems support, and broadcast technology. With the dissolution of DIS, former director Forsythe entered an early partial retirement program at half-time and became a special assistant to the dean; later he had a similar role for Don Gentry. The functions of Distance Learning Services were absorbed into Continuing and Distance Education.

The restructuring also included the creation of a new Office of Communication and Marketing within the Office of Continuing Education and Conferences. This unit incorporated OIELL's communication office and all photographic and graphic arts services that were previously part of the Division of Instructional Services. The Office of Communication and Marketing provided marketing and publications support for OCEC, and it served as OCEC's liaison for to university printing services and photographic services. The unit reported through OCEC Technical Services.

Gentry felt that this restructuring was necessary to take CEC to "the next level" (a Jischke-era catchphrase) and that the new structure would initiate a creative synergy with the staffs of continuing education and conferences working more closely together. After a year of working with this new structure as interim dean, Pagano became the permanent dean of Continuing Education and Conferences in July 2003 after a national search.

The units that were included in the Office of Continuing Education and Conferences under Pagano were as follows:

- Conferences—Paul Horngren, director
- Continuing and Distance Education—Michael Eddy, assistant dean
  - Enrichment programs for seniors (WALLA)—Mary Gardner, manager
  - Evening courses—Barbara Tyner, manager
  - Credit and noncredit professional development programs—Jenny Towler, manager
- The University Calendar Office—Ruth Thompson, manager
- Communications and Technical Services—Robin Jones, manager
- Business Services—Patty Whaley, manager

Strategic Planning

Once Pagano was established as permanent dean, the department embarked on a strategic planning initiative. When Martin Jischke had become president in 2000, strategic planning had become paramount. The university administration spent its first year assembling a plan for the institution. Individual units were expected to develop plans that would support the university plan. The five-year plan OCEC published in 2005 systematically took the major areas of the university plan and developed strategies that would help fulfill university objectives and defined specific metrics by which the success of those strategies would be assessed. The plan demonstrated that OCEC was committed to pursuing the goals that the university had set out. It reinforced OCEC's role as an asset to the university in accomplishing its stated goals.

Financing Evening Classes

An issue that was brought to Pagano's attention almost immediately was the finances of Evening Classes. As noted earlier, the only revenues these classes generated were tuition from part-time, nontraditional students from the community. Full-time students, who had become 80 percent of evening class enrollments, paid for evening classes within their block tuition, upon which OCEC had no claim. In 1994 OCEC was reimbursed for 44 percent of evening class enrollments; by 2001 it was only reimbursed for 21 percent, predictably leading to a deficit for the program. In his 2001–02 unit annual report for Continuing and Distance Education to the dean, Eddy wrote that evening classes were "a continuous financial drain" and recommended that OCEC either discontinue them or "press for a new financial model."

In October 2002 Provost Sally Mason charged Pagano with forming a committee to study the evening class situation and recommend ways to sort out its financial dilemma. On February 10, 2003, the committee submitted its recommendations to Mason and Jim Almond, vice president for Business Services. The committee recommended a recurring allocation of $311,000, which would be sufficient to support about thirty evening classes in the fall and spring terms. Two weeks later a memo approving the proposal was signed by Ken Burns, executive vice president and treasurer, Provost Mason, and President Jischke. In Jischke's signature space was a handwritten note saying, "OK, per discussion w/ KPB [Burns]. Concerned about overload payments to reg. faculty." Overload proved to be an issue that would arise again but was difficult to address at that moment because overload payments had been intrinsic to evening classes. In his memo of April 11 to evening class manager Barb Tyner regarding Fall 2003 salaries for evening classes, Eddy wrote, "Purdue instructors being paid via overload will not be paid in excess of 20 percent of their salary for Evening Class instruction or Evening Class instruction in conjunction with other overload payments," restating the existing overload policy of Executive Memorandum C-18.

Getting Students into Online Classes

Evening classes were a relatively straightforward issue compared to distance learning. The Swain era had established momentum for distance learning as a partnership endeavor through the Indiana College Network (ICN). Despite Swain's efforts, Purdue was not creating courses to be made available through ICN, nor were Purdue students clamoring to enroll in ICN courses offered by partner institutions. In AY 1999–2000 exactly two Purdue West Lafayette students participated in an ICN course.

In AY 1999–2000, Camilla Lawson joined OCEC as manager of OCEC's Purdue Student Learning Center, which was intended to be the hub of ICN activity at Purdue. In her former role as associate registrar, Lawson had participated in the IPSE implementation planning process. She recognized that the availability of distance learning courses from a statewide consortium could help students meet their educational goals. Soon she came to realize that students simply did not have information about ICN because their academic advisors, who guide students in their selection of courses, did not have information about ICN. So, she launched a communications campaign aimed at academic advisers. She had the OCEC webpage modified to list all the ICN courses that were approved for Purdue credit. She became a regular at Purdue Academic Advising Association (PACADA) meetings, answering their questions about distance learning and occasionally making formal presentations. One Lawson memo to the advisors bore the subject line "Helping Your Advisees Achieve Graduation Goals through Distance Learning." The approach implied in that subject line was effective because advisors wanted their advisees to succeed, and the memo made the case that distance learning could help them achieve that. Once that line of communication opened, Purdue student participation grew throughout Pagano's administration, as shown below.

Year	Enrollments	Growth (%)
1999–2000	2	NA
2000–01	333	165
2001–02	1,117	235
2002–03	1,928	73
2003–04	2,646	37
2004–05	3,759	42
2005–06	3,942	5
2006–07	4,481	14
2007–08	4,069	-9
2008–09	5,087	25
2009–10	5,263	3

Growth of 371 percent over nine years was indicative of the demand ICN was fulfilling for Purdue students and the impact of Lawson's efforts to help Purdue students benefit from distance learning.

Addressing Misconceptions about Online Courses

ICN courses were viewed with skepticism by many Purdue faculty. Some was skepticism about the efficacy of online learning generally. There was also skepticism about the true equivalency of courses from other campuses and universities. OCEC procedures required a Purdue equivalency existed or be established with the registrar. In addition, a sign-off by the appropriate department head was required each term before an ICN course section could be established at Purdue. (In 2012 the Indiana legislature passed requirements for a Statewide Transfer General Education Core of at least thirty credit hours, which added some credibility to the free movement of course credits within Indiana higher education.) Purdue departments occasionally requested changes to other institutions' courses before accepting them as equivalents.

Some faculty also voiced the opinion that students who took distance learning courses were weak students looking for an easy way to earn credit for a course. OCEC tested that premise by comparing AY 2005–06 data on Purdue students enrolled in campus-based classes with Purdue students enrolled in IPSE partners' equivalent classes. Students in IPSE sections had a slightly higher grade point average (2.95) than peers in campus-based classes (2.83). Moreover, 3.4 percent of students in campus-based classes were on academic probation, while only .5 percent in IPSE sections were. Other findings were that students in IPSE sections were, on average, 1.7 years older than peers in on-campus classes and were twice as likely to be classified as in their seventh or eighth term than their campus-based peers. That IPSE students were taking courses later in their academic careers suggested that ICN provided a means for them to take courses that they had been unable to take earlier. That they were slightly older might have indicated that more nontraditional students opted for online classes, which would become a problem for evening classes.

Changing the IPSE Financial Model

Though ICN was clearly delivering a service Purdue students needed, it was a costly proposition for the university. In the IPSE financial model, the student's home institution would pay the course host institution 90 percent of its credit-hour tuition. The primary institutions that were providing ICN courses for Purdue students were Ivy Tech and Vincennes University; in 2005–06, 44 percent of Purdue's ICN enrollments went to those institutions. Ninety percent of Purdue's 2004–05 in-state credit-hour tuition was $157.64, while Ivy Tech's equivalent tuition was $80.30, and Vincennes was $101.50. Purdue ICN students generated substantially more revenue for those institutions than their own students.

The logic of reimbursing the originating institution at its own rate rather than that of the student's home institution was clear to Provost Sally Mason, as shown in her memo of April 7, 2010: "The current tuition and fees at public universities presumably reflect the relative costs of instruction at those respective institutions. We believe a more logical business model is to reimburse the originating institutions at a rate that reflects more closely that institution's tuition costs, rather than at the student's home institution rate."

OCEC calculated that its total ICN expenditure in 2005–06 would be $2,484,578 under the then current model. Under the proposed model of paying the host institutions' tuition, Purdue's payout would be $1,667,629, a savings of $816,949.

After much discussion, IPSE's board approved a revision of ICN's Home Institution Model on June 2, 2006, which included the following: "Home institutions will forward 90% of the tuition collected up to 100% of the originating institution's resident or general service per-credit-hour rates. . . . In no case will the Home Institution forward more than 90% of its tuition collected."

The document was circulated to academic and financial officers at the member institutions in early November and was signed by Pagano, Vice Provost for Engagement Vic Lechtenberg (who succeeded Don Gentry in that role), Provost Sally Mason, and Vice President for Business Services Jim Almond. By early spring it was apparent that Ivy Tech and Vincennes University would not sign off on the new model in view of the financial loss it would entail for them. Lechtenberg and Pagano met with the IPSE group on April 11 to work out an arrangement. By this time, the Indiana Commission for Higher Education had taken an interest in the matter, and ICHE Commissioner Ken Sauer attended the meeting with a new proposal.

Sauer noted that the Indiana legislature had allowed for "enrollment adjustment funding" to support state-supported institutions' efforts to grow and make postsecondary education available to more Hoosiers. Purdue and IU were excluded from this funding as "mature" institutions. Up to this point, home institutions had been including ICN enrollments in their own enrollment counts, but it had been the Commission's intention that the originating institutions would be credited with those enrollments and thereby become eligible for state enrollment adjustment funding. These funds would significantly reduce (though not fully eliminate) the loss the originating institutions would incur from the change in the reimbursement model. Since Purdue did not benefit from enrollment adjustment funding, it had no substantive objections. The new model required a new reporting regimen for IPSE member institutions to the Commission, but it was generally acceptable to members, including Ivy Tech and Vincennes, and the model was implemented in Summer 2008.

Building Our Own Online Courses

At the same time OCEC was facilitating this change in the ICN model, it was also making the case that Purdue could save money and better serve its students by developing its own online courses. OCEC's analysis showed that the projected costs of developing and supporting Purdue-originated online courses would be, on average, $250 less than Purdue's cost of placing the student in an ICN course. In 2004 Pagano was able to obtain a three-year general fund commitment of $75,000 per year to develop new Purdue online courses. He also won funding for a coordinator for distance learning. Dennis McElhoe was hired as manager for distance learning and was later promoted to associate director of Continuing and Distance Education.

Provost Mason signaled the progress of this plan to ICN in her April 10, 2007, memo to IHETS interim director Bill Kramer: "Purdue has begun an ambitious program to develop a series of Purdue-originated replacement courses for those currently being taught by other originating institutions and that have high Purdue student enrollments." This caused consternation among IPSE partners because Purdue was providing about 70 percent of ICN's cross-institutional enrollments.

The implementation plan was straightforward: In the spring of 2005 OCEC would circulate a request for proposals to develop online courses among departments and develop a subset of proposed courses. At the same time OCEC would actively pursue the development of online versions of the ICN courses that enrolled the most Purdue students. OCEC would provide instructional design support for Purdue instructors and would pay instructors one month's summer salary to develop a course. It would become *de facto* OCEC policy that Purdue online sections would be filled before any Purdue student would be enrolled in an equivalent ICN course. The faculty responded to the RFP with fifteen course proposals, of which OCEC was able to fund eight; some faculty members decided to proceed with course development even without OCEC funding. These courses raised the total of online courses offered by Purdue from five in Fall 2004 to twenty in the fall of 2005.

The letter of agreement OCEC used with departments for course development provided for one semester of development aided and coordinated by OCEC's instructional development specialist, Tianhong Shi. The agreement required the academic department to offer the online course at least three times. It also required that the online course sections be in addition to existing classroom sections, not replacing them, because the logic of offering online classes was to increase access. OCEC would provide a stipend for the development of the course and would cover the instructional costs as it was taught. It was hoped that online courses would generate enough revenues from students at other ICN partner institutions for the courses to be financially self-supporting after three offerings. Such outcomes were rare, however; cross-registration into Purdue-originated courses was a trickle.

Purdue's block tuition created a challenge for generating revenues to support online courses. At most other ICN institutions, students paid by the credit hour, so that new revenue was generated whenever a student enrolled in a course. This was not the case with full-time Purdue–West Lafayette students because of block tuition. Consequently, other ICN partners saw online courses as an opportunity to generate revenues, including Purdue's own regional campuses. One regional campus set up special online sections of business and technical writing courses for Purdue West Lafayette to enroll in through ICN. These sections filled regularly and were revenue generators for the regional campus. The regionals, Ivy Tech, and Vincennes saw financial benefits from Purdue–West Lafayette students in their online courses and were not eager to see the West Lafayette campus grow its online offerings.

That growth did not come easily, however, despite OCEC support and incentives. Many faculty were skeptical of the quality of online instruction and were better rewarded for efforts in research than in course development. Older faculty were not comfortable with the technology, and younger faculty were absorbed with earning tenure. Some graduate instructors were interested in adding online teaching to their resumes, but OCEC was reluctant to turn development responsibility over to them because of their transient nature.

The development of business and technical writing courses showed the elements that needed to be aligned for courses to come together. English 420, Business Writing, and English 421, Technical Writing, were two of the top ICN enrollment classes. One of the two courses was required for many campus majors, so the demand was high.

The English Department couldn't offer enough sections to satisfy the demand, so there was a waiting list for both and many ICN sections. The courses came late in a student's curriculum, so the inability to enroll in a section could delay a student's graduation. Eddy and McElhoe met with English Department head Irwin Weiser multiple times, but he was uncomfortable with the concept. However, Prof. Jim Blakeslely, who oversaw both courses, was eager to explore the technology and saw an opportunity to provide online teaching experience for the department's graduate students. He was able to move Weiser to agree to 420 in 2005 and 421 in 2006 with Blakesley in the lead for online sections development. English 420 was OCEC's first major success in developing a course that was in high demand in ICN.

Negotiations to develop other high-demand courses to replace ICN courses were rarely as successful as those with the English Department. Other high-demand ICN courses included Sociology 100, History 104, Physics 219, Psychology 120, Communications 212, and Political Science 130. In some cases OCEC agreed to develop other courses first or in addition to the target course. In some instances contracted courses simply didn't materialize. So when Prof. Mickey Latour was hired for the new OCEC position of associate dean for distance learning in 2010, he moved away from negotiating individual courses with department heads and faculty members and instead negotiated a "bulk" development arrangement with Joann Miller, associate dean of Liberal Arts, to provide the Liberal Arts courses that OCEC needed for a fixed amount of money. Latour's arrangement transferred instructional reimbursements to the dean's office to be distributed as the dean determined. This allowed the dean to leverage OCEC funding to negotiate with heads for other priorities the heads desired, not just additional salary for instructors. This strategy opened doors that had been closed and resulted in the development of many courses OCEC desired and the addition of needed course sections. Those changes resulted in a spike in Purdue students enrolling in Purdue-originated online courses (from 2,500 in 2009–10 to 8,451 in 2011–12) and a precipitous decline in the number of Purdue West Lafayette students in ICN courses (from 5,263 in 2009–10 to 1,289 in 2011–12), while the overall number of Purdue students taking online courses continued to grow (from 7,763 in 2009–10 to 9,740 in 2011–12). The table below tracks these dynamics for the first decade of the 2000s.

Year	ICN Enrollments	Purdue-Originated Enrollments
2000–01	333	NA
2001–02	1,117	NA
2002–03	1,928	37
2003–04	2,646	140
2004–05	3,759	130
2005–06	3,942	763
2006–07	4,481	1,230
2007–08	4,069	2,608
2008–09	5,087	2,505
2009–10	5,263	2,500
2010–11	3,746	4,103
2011–12	1,289	8,451

In Spring 2011 Pagano announced his target for the next academic year:: "Our goal is by 2012–13 to create capacity for 10,000 enrollments in online courses for Purdue West Lafayette students. We want at least 60 percent of those enrollments in courses originating at Purdue. The remaining capacity would be available through partner institutions in the Indiana College Network consortium" (Purdue News Service 2011a). At the time he was speaking, 87 percent of the Purdue students in online courses were already taking Purdue-originated courses.

"Mainstreaming" OCEC-Administered Classes

In 2005 a study was commissioned by Pagano, university comptroller John Shipley, and Doug Christiansen, assistant vice president for enrollment management and dean of admissions, to determine if credit programs administered through OCEC could be "mainstreamed," which consisted primarily of collecting student fees through the Bursar's Office rather than OCEC. A task force was set up to explore this question, including OCEC personnel and Business Office administrators.

Historically, OCEC had served as registrar and bursar of the programs it administered. The reasons for this were myriad, but they boiled down to the fact that to serve nontraditional students, departments had to develop programs that served their needs, and part of OCEC's mission was to make square programs fit into round administrative slots. In the legacy system, OCEC was treated as a separate campus (Campus 4), which allowed for some flexibility but also created some challenges in that these students were not viewed as part of the "main campus" and had difficulty accessing university resources and privileges. Providing appropriate service to nontraditional students in nontraditional programs required some *ad hoc* solutions, often involving manual workarounds and the cooperation of many offices on campus. Here are a few examples:

> *Availability of financial aid.* To be considered eligible for financial aid, students enrolled in OCEC–administered degree programs had to be visible to both the registrar's and bursar's systems as a Campus 1 student. OCEC students were always in the registrar's system, but because they paid their fees and tuition to OCEC rather than the bursar, they were placed in a "hold fees" file to prevent them from being passed to the bursar's system for fee assessment. When the Bursar's Office was notified by the Division of Financial Aid of an aid-eligible OCEC student, the Bursar's Office requested that the Office of the Registrar remove that student from their "hold fees" file so the student would be passed to the Bursar's Office for fee assessment. The Bursar's Office put a hold on the invoice to prevent it from being mailed in error while it was reviewed. Bursar's Office staff then manually adjusted the fees to the correct amount as per OCEC's rate approval.

Calculation of refunds. The university refund policy was based on a standardized start date, fees, and course length. When a student required a refund for a OCEC program that started at mid-semester, lasted only a week, or charged a nonstandard fee, the refund had to be calculated by OCEC staff and submitted to the bursar for custom handling.

Payment options. OCEC-administered credit programs offered market-driven payment options that were not available through the bursar. These included third-party payments (usually by the student's employer), installment payment plans, and payment by credit card. (The bursar's system did not allow credit card payments for fees at that time.) "Mainstreaming" OCEC-administered programs would add a significant burden to the Bursar's Office and rescinding these payment options would significantly damage the programs' market position.

These processes, and others like them, were cumbersome and required the cooperation of many campus administrative units, but mainstreaming the programs would put the entire burden on already challenged offices and would require complex changes to the existing legacy system. After several months of meetings, the mainstreaming task force submitted a recommendation that changes to how OCEC credit programs were administered be deferred until the university adopted the new Enterprise Resource Planning (ERP) system, as was beginning to be discussed, rather than attempting to accommodate OCEC services with difficult changes to the legacy system.

Converting to the Banner System

It was clear that OCEC would have much at stake in the new ERP system as the university began seriously exploring its options. Four prospective ERP vendors were invited to campus to give demonstrations of their products. Their demos covered several student scenarios that vendors were asked to show how their systems would handle. One scenario was of a student enrolled in an online degree program (specifically the veterinary technology associate degree program). Several OCEC administrators, program coordinators, and Business Office staff attended the demos and submitted vendor evaluations. Eventually STC Banner won the contract.

The Banner implementation project was branded OnePurdue because it represented an integration of all the university's business and student-management systems. Initially there was an intention to incorporate all of Purdue's campuses into OnePurdue, but eventually that evolved into separate instances of the system. The OnePurdue implementation was a massive project. About three hundred Purdue employees were reassigned for a three-year period to work exclusively with the project. Those employees were relocated to a building in the Research Park. OCEC had regular meetings with a team that had been assigned to deal with OCEC-administered programs. Generally, these meetings included individuals from the Bursar's Office and the Registrar's Office as well as OCEC. In the implementation, "Campus 4" of the legacy system disappeared and OCEC programs were recognized as a sub-campus of West Lafayette. The sub-campus designation allowed for flexibility with the calendar and with fees. The adopted arrangements are far too complex to summarize here, but suffice to say that when OnePurdue went live in July 2008 for Fall registration, things generally came off well. With some exceptions, participants in online degree programs were billed the correct amounts at the right times. Refinement of the system allowed for greater flexibility over the next several years, and ultimately OCEC courses and programs were well served by the new system. OCEC-administered courses and programs became more "mainstreamed," which is to say that payments were generally made to the Bursar's Office and transfers were made back to OCEC to cover its administrative expenses.

OnePurdue did not incorporate OCEC's noncredit activities, including conferences and noncredit distance learning programs. Nor did it eliminate all manual processes. For example, international students coming to campus were required to produce evidence of insurance. That requirement made little sense for online international students who would never step foot on campus. However, Banner did not offer a means to distinguish these students, so each academic term, OCEC had to manually produce a list of online-only international students who should not receive communications regarding insurance requirements and share it with the Student Hospital staff that oversaw insurance, who would then manually delete them from their distribution list.

A Provost's Distance Learning Task Force

In 2008 Provost Randy Woodson authorized Pagano to establish a task force on distance learning to determine how to move Purdue to the next level. The twelve-person task force consisted of three faculty members, five Business Office administrators, and the registrar. One academic dean participated. Assistant Provost Nancy Bulger cochaired with Pagano. The OCEC contingent consisted of Pagano, Eddy, and business manager Patty Whaley. The group met first on November 17, 2008, and met biweekly through the 2009 Spring term. Its charge was threefold:

- To develop an appropriate funding model for online learning
- To provide an academic framework for future online course development at Purdue
- To make recommendations to provide synergies between online course offerings, evening courses, and summer school to optimize student, faculty, and staff success.

The information gathering related to this project was extensive. OCEC staff participated in three daylong benchmarking trips to peer institutions that were considered ahead of Purdue in their online development: Penn State, University of Georgia, and Western Michigan.

In February 2009, the National Association of State Universities and Land-Grant Colleges and the Sloan Consortium released the results of a survey of more than ten thousand faculty members and administrators at sixty-seven public campuses about their opinions on distance learning. Sloan offered to provide Purdue with a cut of their data from over 640 Purdue personnel who completed the survey and to compare their responses to the national results. Sloan sent a representative to campus to present the Purdue data to the task force. The results were sobering. About 35 percent of national respondents said they had taught an online course; about 20 percent of Purdue respondents had. About 35 percent of national respondents had developed an online course; 20 percent of Purdue respondents had. These figures suggested that Purdue was behind peer institutions in incorporating distance learning. Purdue and national respondents shared the belief that teaching online required more effort than traditional classroom teaching (55 percent Purdue, 65 percent national). Over 70 percent of Purdue respondents felt the learning outcomes of online courses were inferior to face-to-face courses. Motivations for online teaching were led by providing more flexible access for students and online being the best way to reach particular students, with over 50 percent agreement. Barriers scoring above 50 percent included additional effort to develop and deliver, lack of student self-discipline, inadequate compensation, and lack of credit in tenure/promotion decisions. The only area of institutional support that Purdue respondents rated above average was technological infrastructure at 45 percent; the lowest-rated was incentives for delivering (teaching) online, with 12 percent rating it above average.

OCEC conducted its own survey of Purdue deans and academic department heads. The survey elicited a 53 percent response rate. When asked how important distance learning was to their units' strategic goals, 53 percent reported that it was important or very important. Regarding the value of distance learning on a scale of 1 to 5, the strongest responses were for expanding access to new students (3.94), keeping up with competitors (3.73), providing flexibility for traditional students (3.63), and generating income (3.12). Sixty-two percent said their units were likely or very likely to develop new online courses. Their plans were fairly evenly divided as to level of online course work: lower-level undergraduate (2.98 on a scale of 5), upper-level undergraduate (3.04), and graduate (3.26). Fifty-four percent reported that they had plans to offer specific programs or courses in the next three to five years. Seventy-nine percent expected online teaching to be treated as part of the normal teaching load, not overload. Sixty percent looked to the university for funding of distance learning. Other open-ended questions provided the task force with useful information about what expenses they anticipated for distance learning for development and ongoing, how they might utilize revenues generated by distance learning offerings, and how the university could best support their efforts in this area. The OCEC survey provided granular information about how key players on campus were thinking about distance learning.

The eleven-page task force report recommended many actions to be taken either by the university or by OCEC. The covering memo of the report, submitted to Provost Woodson on September 21, 2009, summarized the recommendations as follows:

1. Elevate the stature/visibility of online learning at Purdue, and position it and name it in such a way to reflect the mission and stature.
2. Structure the online learning support system into two crucial focal areas:
   a. Continuation of support for undergraduate students through offering high-demand courses online to facilitate access and reduce time to degree completion. Utilize a balanced mix of both Purdue and IPSE partner-originated courses.
   b. Centralized support to stimulate entrepreneurial efforts to launch professional master's degrees and other credentialing in areas of Purdue strength and demonstrated demand.
3. Initiate a financial model such that funds generated from online course course/program are used to incentivize the activities by directing them back to the department (to reduce dependence on overload payments to faculty).
4. Provide for sufficient resources centrally to fund administrative and technical support to accommodate online growth activities.
5. Develop a five-year growth plan for both areas of focus, with accompanying metrics and targets.

The report recommended dozens of actions that we will not repeat here. Significant activities and policy changes that resulted from the report included the following:

- The launching of an internal search for an associate dean for distance learning who would provide leadership in carrying out the goals enumerated by the task force. The result of the search was the hiring of Mickey Latour, professor of animal science and the developer/instructor of a highly successful online course.
- The acquisition and development of new space for distance learning operations in the ground floor of Stewart Center. The previous space was 1,431 square feet, while the new learning center was 2,718 square feet and included one of the largest dedicated testing facilities on campus.
- The development of a "response team" to coordinate university-level administrative activity around the initiation of new distance learning programs. It would include administrators from Student Services, Enrollment Management, Business Services, the Graduate School, and OCEC. Its chief function would be communicative to ensure that no "surprises" sprang up that would delay or block the launch of new programs.
- The movement away from overload payments to individual faculty members in favor of transferring funds to departments to distribute according to their priorities. This addressed the concern expressed by Provost Mason and President Jischke about overload payments to faculty for teaching. Perhaps more importantly

it helped align continuing education programming with the goals of academic departments and colleges rather than the interests of individual faculty members.
- The establishment of market-based pricing for programs. The report recommended that online programs should be "offered on a self-supporting basis with revenues covering all costs, both direct and administrative." It also allowed that pricing of programs "should be market-based, taking into consideration demand, competition, and costs." Pricing at rates other than Purdue's board-approved tuition and fees could be established through a special rate request process through OCEC and with the authorization of the Treasurer. It also allowed new programs a three-to-five-year window to establish financial viability.
- The rebranding of the Office for Continuing Education and Conferences to Extended University. Eddy's team had researched names of units delivering online learning at twenty other public institutions. Only five retained some version of "continuing education." The most frequent formulation was the name of the university and "online," as in "U of I Online" and "OSU Online." Three institutions included some for "extension" in their branding: UC Berkeley Extension Online, New Mexico State's College of Extended Learning, and Oregon State's Extended Campus. Though the task force recommended a rebranding, the actual process was administrative, and those administrators arrived at "Purdue Extended Campus." When the name change was announced in March 2011 Pagano said, "Extended Campus captures the essence of our mission. Purdue is not a place fixed on a map. This is a university without borders that serves people who can't come to campus for a variety of reasons. The Conference Division, which brings almost 80,000 professionals and members of organizations from across the world to campus each year, also hosts events on five other continents. Additionally, 31,000 people enrolled in distance learning activities sponsored by Purdue departments last year" (Purdue News Service, 2011b). The new name was widely embraced by staff and on the campus. The branding harkened back to early twentieth century when "continuing education" and "extension" were almost synonymous. It also reflected the broad concept of "extension" as outreach and community engagement embraced by Don Brown nearly thirty years before.
- Engaging an online program management firm to help Purdue move forward with online degree programs. The report recommended that "OCEC should evaluate the services of a third-party vendor to help faculty develop, market, launch, support and manage distance learning programs." A large working group of faculty and administrators was established to create a request for proposals to be distributed to companies by Purchasing, to evaluate the proposals, and eventually to select a vendor for Purdue to work with. The request for proposals elicited nine proposals that resulted in three firms being invited to campus. From the three, Deltak of Oakbrook, Illinois, was selected, and a five-year exclusive contract was negotiated with them. Deltak's impact on the growth of online programs will be discussed later.

The online learning task force report laid out a structure for administering online learning courses for campus students and programs that would attract working professionals. That structure worked effectively for many years.

North Central Accreditation Process

In conjunction with Purdue's ten-year reaccreditation by the Higher Learning Commission of the North Central Association of Colleges and Schools, Pagano was selected in 2009 to cochair the university accreditation steering committee with Christine Ladisch, vice provost for academic affairs. This committee oversaw the internal self-study groups that focused on the five criteria for accreditation. The self-study document provided baseline information for the peer evaluators who visited campus for three days in March 2010. The accreditation was a two-year endeavor, and while it was not directly related to continuing education programming, Pagano's appointment and the work he did for the accreditation process reflected well on the status of extended education on the campus.

In August 2011 Mark Pagano was named provost and vice chancellor for academic affairs at Montana State University, Billings. In his decade of leading OCEC/PEC much had been accomplished. Swain had set a course for distance learning to be the dominant means by which outreach education would be delivered. Pagano oversaw the creation of infrastructure of policy, services, and finance that created the conditions for impressive growth in Purdue distance learning programming and participation.

7

2011–2015

Mark pagano departed purdue university in September 2011 to become the provost and academic vice chancellor of Montana State University, Billings. Upon his departure, Mary A. Sadowski was named interim dean of Purdue Extended Campus (PEC). Before being appointed interim dean, Sadowski had been an associate dean in the Polytechnic Institute (formerly the College of Technology) and held an appointment as professor of computer graphics in that college. During her time as interim dean, Sadowski reported to Dale Whitaker, vice provost for undergraduate academic affairs, and to Suresh Garimella, associate vice president for engagement, a continuation of the dual reporting line that had begun in Pagano's tenure.

A search advisory committee was appointed by Provost Tim Sands to identify a permanent dean for PEC. The committee was chaired by Victor Lechtenberg, special assistant to the president and director of the Center for Regional Development. The committee was composed of fifteen faculty and staff members from across campus. Sadowski was ultimately selected to become the permanent dean of Purdue Extended Campus in May 2012.

It was clear from the outset that the focus of Sadowski's tenure as Extended Campus dean was to be on distance/online learning. In the news release announcing her permanent appointment, Provost Sands said, "Mary has a deep understanding of the important role Extended Campus plays in a range of educational efforts, particularly in continuing education and distance learning." Sadowski was quoted as saying, "I'm excited to lead Extended Campus, which offers so many vital programs. . . . Online learning is becoming very important in today's world. We are increasing the resources and efforts we are devoting to this key area." In summarizing the responsibilities of Extended Campus, the release said, "In addition to distance education, the continuing education unit provides enrichment programs for seniors, evening courses, and credit and noncredit professional development programs" (Purdue News Service 2012a). The department's conference operation was not noted, though it was in the PEC unit.

Most online learning at Purdue was supported by PEC during this time. This approach was expanding and evolving rapidly, with online content delivery platforms that were augmented by integrated tools for online assessment, simulation, student interaction, and faculty engagement (Purdue News Service 2012a).

During Sadowski's time as dean, Purdue Extended Campus included the following units, as described by Sadowski in her presentation to the Board of Trustees' Academic Affairs Committee (Sadowski 2013).

Conferences—Director, Geni Greiner

1. Year-round conference and meeting services were planned and administered for faculty, staff, and students.
2. The conference coordinators handled all aspects of these programs (including registration, revenue, lodging, food and beverage, meeting space, and expense management).
3. Conferences handled 650 programs both on and off campus that totaled seventy thousand participants in 2012.

Online Education—Director, Michael Eddy

1. Online courses for degree-seeking students
   a. PEC supported undergraduate online courses that created the opportunity for students to take online courses that decreased the time to graduation.
2. Online degrees and certificate programs
   a. PEC oversaw the financial and other administrative aspects of Engineering Continuing Education (College of Engineering) and ProStar (College of Technology master's degrees and certificates).
   b. PEC coordinated Purdue's relationship with Deltak, a third-party service provider for online programs.
3. Noncredit Programs
   a. PEC assisted academic departments that provide programing to help professionals maintain their certification or licensure to practice.
   b. PEC provided administrative support for noncredit programs of greater length and substance that usually address organizations' needs to develop new skill sets within their workforce.
   c. PEC helped Purdue experiment with Massive Open Online Courses (MOOCs), free online courses designed for mass participation.

Online Learning and the Decadal Funding Plan

During Sadowski's interim year of 2011, Provost Sands had projected online learning as an element in his decadal funding plan. The plan was put forth in the context of falling support of the university from the state and reductions in federal research funding. The decadal plan was to remove financial planning from the year-to-year approach and project new revenue streams that would be more reliable than the current ones. In his presentation at the Presidential Leadership Forum of September 7, 2011, Sands laid out an overview of the decadal plan. It's goal was to "identify new resource opportunities that will enhance the excellence and reputation of all aspects of the university's mission, and alleviate reliance on student tuition and fees and state appropriations." Its opportunities and threats analysis identified expanding Purdue's online presence as one of five opportunity areas. Growth could occur through "big ideas," which Sands identified as "Efficient and Effective Purdue, Innovative Purdue, and Global Purdue." The plan placed "Expanding Purdue Online" as a function of Global Purdue (though PEC staff would have seen online as contributing to all three areas). The plan envisioned an expanded Purdue online creating a global network; building new industry, government, institution, and research partnerships; offering degree programs; and supporting lifelong learning. (Sands's presentation slides are available at https://www.yumpu.com/en/document/read/25596587/provost-priorities-and-decadal-funding-plan-purdue-university.)

The decadal plan's view of online learning's role at Purdue was ambitious and integral to its model for growth. The plan placed what had been considered a marginal enterprise near the center of the University's model for fiscal stability. That change represented a major step forward for online learning, but it also created a challenging environment for the new PEC dean. Elevating online learning meant many institutional players would become more involved in it than had ever been the case.

Year of the MOOC and Mitch

The year 2012 was a particularly charged one for online learning, which became almost synonymous with Massive Open Online Courses, or MOOCs. On November 4, in a headline, the New York Times declared 2012 "the Year of the MOOC" (Pappano 2012). While the idea of the large-scale open online courses had been around for a while, MOOCs exploded when Stanford professor Sebastian Thrun's artificial intelligence course attracted 150,000 enrollments worldwide in the fall of 2011. By the fall of 2012 Harvard's and MIT's nonprofit platform for MOOCs called EdX had attracted over 370,000 enrollments in its first offerings. The for-profit platform Coursera, founded by Stanford professor Andrew Ng, had attracted 1.7 million enrollments to MOOCs offered by thirty-three high profile universities, including Princeton, Brown, Columbia, and Duke. Some professors teaching in these massive courses were teaching more students in a single MOOC than they had taught in their entire careers. The academic world was abuzz with this "disruptive" phenomenon, and questions were beginning to be raised about how Purdue would participate in it.

By chance, 2012 was also the year that Purdue was transitioning to a new president. Then governor Mitch Daniels, whose term in office was expiring, would drive his Harley Davidson up from Indianapolis to campus for his "orientation" to Purdue. This consisted of days of multiple sessions on various topics. The first two-hour session of his first day of orientation was about online learning at Purdue. PEC understood that Daniels had requested the timing of this session. Representatives of the various units participating in online learning—Engineering, Technology, Management, PEC, and ITaP— planned a detailed presentation for the new president with each group presenting for an allotted period. However, as soon as the first speaker began, Daniels began peppering her with questions, and the structure of the presentation became largely moot. It was apparent that online learning would be a major interest of the Daniels administration.

Hub-U: A Purdue Answer to MOOCs

On May 11, 2012, the University announced the formation of Purdue HUB-U, an online education initiative expected to extend from Purdue classrooms to around the planet. The initiative was based on HubZero, a Purdue-developed online course platform. The administrative home for the HubU initiative was Purdue's NanoHUB, a National Science Foundation–funded international nanotechnology resource with 450,000 visitors and 218,000 engaged users. A two-part pilot course, "Basic Concepts of Nanoelectronics," taught by Prof. Supriyo Datta, had been taught on the HubZero platform. It had attracted 900 students from twenty-seven countries. The majority were graduate students or industry professionals, most of whom paid thirty dollars for the class and a certificate of completion. What distinguished HubZero from other course platforms was the computing power that was incorporated into it so that learners could participate in complex simulations without resorting to external software. Sands saw the initiative as far-reaching and comprehensive. He stated that he expected its "modular approach to coursework [would] allow the same content to be adapted in a flexible manner across a wide range of delivery formats, ranging from blended learning for on-campus courses to low-cost, low-touch programs available to individuals and institutions" (Purdue News Service 2012b). HubU represented Purdue's approach to MOOCs—short-term courses offered on a global scale that could be offered inexpensively at a high volume because they were "low-touch"—that is, designed so that little input was required of the faculty instructor after the course was built and implemented.

Sands had arranged for HubU to be supported with a $2 million development fund. The initiative was expected to break even in five years. In the announcement President France Cordova said that HubU "would augment Purdue Extended Campus, the university's central resource for distance education activities for credit and continuing education" (Purdue News Service 2012b). The announcement about HubU was released the day after the announcement that Sadowski had been named dean of PEC. HubU, rebranded as PurdueNext, would not come under PEC administration until 2017.

A Presidential Forum on Online Learning

On October 2, 2012, then acting president Sands devoted a presidential forum to online learning. The intent was to provide faculty and staff with a perspective on the various approaches and models for online learning. The forum included a panel consisting of Sadowski; Prof. Tim Newby, who was directing a highly successful online master's program in educational technology; Dale Harris, the director of Continuing Engineering Education; and Prof. Ananth Iyer, whom Sands had appointed as the director of HubU. The forum was held in Stewart Center's Fowler Hall and was attended by about 150 faculty and staff members. As he had done earlier, Sands framed the discussion around the revenue potential of online learning. Noting that federal support for research was down significantly and that state support for the university was also decreasing, he indicated that online learning was a potential revenue source to make up for some of these losses without generating major expenses of its own. Other panelists supported this view. During the question period one faculty member expressed that the online course platform, then Blackboard, was not reliable. Another also indicated that weaker students were attracted to online delivery and did not fare well with it because of lack of self-discipline. Newby noted that Deltak student services representatives helped his students stay engaged, contacting them if they had not logged into their courses in some time and keeping professors informed of such issues. Sands introduced MOOCs as another mode of online learning, one that could expand Purdue's global reach and reputation and allowed faculty to teach thousands of students. He encouraged the audience to consider how MOOCs could serve their departments and to be timely about it: "There's talk that if you're not in the game, you're going to miss the wave" (Sparger 2012). A few days later Sands's wave metaphor would come back to him in another form.

The Board of Trustees Gets Interested in Online Learning

The October 2012 meeting of the Board of Trustees was a watershed moment for online learning at Purdue in that it made clear that the university trustees were aware of the broad strokes of the developments in online learning and were very interested in Purdue's prospective involvement in it. According to the minutes of the meeting, Sands reported on the open forum he and Sadowski had conducted about "the future of, and the university's priorities for, online education." The minutes read, "Following President Sands' report, Chairman Krach remarked that the Board sees online education as a tsunami. He encouraged President Sands to develop guiding principles that will aid in building a cohesive strategy for online education at Purdue." The metaphor of the tsunami was highly charged, indicating that the Board viewed online learning less as an opportunity and more as a potentially overwhelming threat to the university that needed to be dealt with to avoid disaster.

The *Exponent*'s coverage of the meeting rendered the exchange between Krach and Sands somewhat more dramatically than the minutes had.

> Acting president Tim Sands gave a report about topics ranging from the need for online courses in Purdue's future to the current environment of higher education.
>
> Sands spoke about the benefits of Mass Open Online Courses being incorporated into the Purdue education, and the need to "put stakes in the ground."
>
> Sands was asked by Board of Trustees chairman Keith Krach whether there was a date or strategic plan set for such courses yet.
>
> "No, not yet," Sands responded. "Right now, what we're doing is a lot of experiments, but we're going to be pushing on all fronts." (Staff Reports 2012)

The *Exponent* reporter didn't note Krach's tsunami metaphor, but it is clear that Sands viewed MOOCs as an opportunity to be explored rather than a threatening tidal wave.

From the perspective of Extended Campus, MOOCs were a new element in an already established environment of online learning at Purdue that consisted of hundreds of online classes for campus students, a growing number of online master's degree programs, and several noncredit training programs intended for working professionals. PEC's concern was how MOOCs would fit into that spectrum. Could MOOCs be combined or sequenced so that they might be viewed as the equivalent of a credit course? Could they be used as a "free sample" to ease students into online degree or certificate programs? Could the MOOC model be used with a modest fee to ramp up noncredit professional learning to a massive scale?

Sadowski was invited to present on Purdue Extended Campus to the Board of Trustees' Academic Affairs Committee on April 4, 2013. Coordinating with Sands, she prepared a presentation that covered the entire range of PEC's activities including conferences, evening classes, and noncredit programs, as well as online classes and online degree programs. It presented a three-part strategy for online learning in PEC:

- Retain students and graduate them in a timely manner. Develop and offer online courses focused on the needs of undergraduate students
- Expand graduate studies. Promote and support online master's degrees for working professionals
- Enhance technical skill sets. Administer online noncredit training programs for professionals in Indiana, nationally, globally. (Academic Affairs Committee Meeting Minutes, August 4, 2013, https://earchives.lib.purdue.edu/digital/collection/bot/id/52862/rec/1294)

The strategic priorities Sadowski outlined reflected what PEC was currently pursuing. The presentation also included ten-year projections for growth in undergraduate online courses, graduate programs, noncredit professional training (focusing on Hub-U), and MOOCs. The presentation was not the full-blown strategic plan Krach had asked about; it was a description of what PEC had been authorized to do by the university and a projection of how PEC would incrementally grow those initiatives.

The October 2012 Board of Trustees meeting had set an agenda for Sadowski and Extended Campus to work with the president (soon to be Mitch Daniels) and the new administration to develop a plan for online learning for Purdue, presumably at the system level. Such a plan would need to address the coming "tsunami" of MOOCs but also how online education in general would fit into Purdue's academic future. This expansive mission was challenging for Sadowski because PEC had been built to facilitate initiatives set by the administration and to make those initiatives work in an environment that had not been structured for them. PEC had not been designed to envision an agenda and to drive that agenda within the university. It was also challenging in that, though trustees and upper administrators felt compelled to address the disruption of online education, their vision was not transparent and still evolving.

STATE AUTHORIZATION OF ONLINE LEARNING

In 2011, as distance learning was booming throughout the country and starting to make its mark at Purdue, the US Department of Education (DoE) initiated a new policy that set the distance learning community at universities scrambling. In March, the DoE issued a "Dear Colleague" letter reminding administrators of distance learning programs that the states have authority to regulate the offering of distance learning programs by out-of-state institutions to residents in their state. Institutions that could not demonstrate that they had proper state authorization for their programs would be required to return federal financial aid for students in states where authorization had not been granted. In addition, the DoE "retains the ability to take other actions against noncompliant institutions." The DoE rule had initially indicated that institutions should be compliant by July 1, 2011, but the March letter allowed that for the 2011–12 academic year institutions would be considered making a "good faith effort" to become compliant if

- "The institution has applied for approval of its offerings in such a State, either in response to the publication of the regulations, or earlier if the State notified the institution that such approval was required;
- The institution is able to document its application for approval and the application's receipt by the State; and
- The institution notifies the Department when the State issues its decision on the pending applications for approval."

A subsequent letter in July extended the enforcement date to July 1, 2014. Then in July 2011 the US District Court for the District of Columbia vacated the distance education portion of the state authorization regulations on a procedural basis; the ruling was upheld by the US Court of Appeals in June 2012. Because the court ruling was procedural, it was expected that DoE would correct the matter in time. Moreover, DoE reminded universities that there was still the expectation that they would be in compliance with state rules. Since the federal rules were under Title IV, the federal financial aid program, administrators were very concerned not to endanger their ability to grant federal aid (Poulin and Boeke n.d.).

The situation for the federal regulations was chaotic and threw distance education administrators into something of a panic that was reflected in numerous sessions at national conferences and well-attended teleconferences on home campuses. The time frame was a moving target and the rules themselves seemed on-again-off-again. DoE implied that it was merely enforcing existing rules, but it had always been understood that if an institution wished to have a physical presence in another state, either bricks-and-mortar or a face-to-face instructional environment, permission from the state would be required. But generally, distance learning had not been considered a "presence." In fact, one could argue that it was no different than a state resident deciding to attend an out-of-state university, but virtually.

Many states saw the availability of out-of-state distance learning programs as a threat to their own universities' programs. Some made the authorization process onerous by requiring program administrators to appear in person before authorizing bodies in the state. Some charged very substantial fees. There were fifty different sets of rules and they were changing to adapt to the new environment; DoE was not offering to provide a centralized database of those requirements. The authorizations were for individual programs, not for institutions, and the authorizations were generally for only one year. Nor was there any minimum number of students from a given state: if a program had one student from a state, authorization was required. Since the offering institution had no way of predicting what states students would apply from, the only practical course was to seek authorizations in all states. None of the states were equipped to deal with the volume of authorization requests that would be generated. To add to the challenge, authorization had to be obtained based on what state the student was in at the time of instruction. Universities had information about students' state of residence, but none regarding their whereabouts as they took courses. (Someone labeled this policy "residency by GPS.")

In 2011 Sadowski directed Eddy to begin documenting progress toward compliance on state authorization in a series of biannual reports submitted to the vice president for ethics and compliance, Alysa Rollock. These reports were intended to document Purdue's "good faith effort" toward compliance, and they continued through 2013. In 2014 Sadowski hired Julia Kalish as interim associate dean to coordinate PEC's response to state authorization on a one-year temporary appointment. By the end of fiscal 2014–15, Kalish could document that Purdue was authorized to offer online programs to residents in all states but five: Alabama, Arkansas, Maryland, Massachusetts, and Mississippi. In his year-end report to Associate Provost Frank Dooley, Eddy (then serving as acting director) noted that those five states had "made it either too expensive or too difficult to gain authorization, so the appropriate path seems to be to inform our client departments to either stop recruiting in those states or seek authorization on their own." Some programs began posting notices that they could not accept students from states in which the programs were noncompliant. In the

2014–15 report, Eddy also recommended that a permanent position be established to coordinate state authorization. In 2015, Tanisha Willoughby, an attorney from Indianapolis, was hired into that role. Her appointment was split with the Office of Ethics and Compliance, directed by Vice President Alysa Rollock.

Reciprocity Agreements Ease State-Authorization Complexities

As it became increasingly clear that state authorization would be nearly unmanageable on a program-by-program basis with fifty ever-changing sets of rules, serious discussions about reciprocity among states began to arise. These discussions ultimately resulted in a comprehensive pact called the State Authorization Reciprocity Agreement (SARA). It began with Lumina Foundation funding the President's Forum (an organization of college and university presidents committed to reinventing higher education) and the Council of State Governments to develop a model reciprocity agreement. Regional higher education compacts—the Western Interstate Commission for Higher Education, Midwestern Higher Education Compact, New England Board of Higher Education, and Southern Regional Education Board—emerged, built on the President's Forum/CSG model to develop regional reciprocity agreements. In August 2013, Lumina Foundation provided funds to the newly established National Council for State Reciprocity Agreements for regional and national implementation. Higher education compacts began inviting states to participate in SARA in January 2014, and on February 21, 2014, Indiana became the first state to join SARA with approval from the Midwestern Higher Education Compact.

Under SARA, states would agree to a universal authorization regimen that would be built around institutions rather than individual programs and would be coordinated by states' higher education commissions or boards. Institutions would apply to their state board to join SARA and the state boards would ensure compliance. State boards would work with out-of-state institutions to resolve problems their students were encountering. Institutions would pay a nominal amount to their state board for the administration of SARA. Ultimately forty-nine states, the District of Columbia, Puerto Rico, and the US Virgin Islands joined SARA, with over 2,100 colleges and universities participating. SARA brought stability and order to state authorization.

System-Wide Courses

The university became interested in exploring how online learning might be administered at the system level. The question was framed in terms of efficiency: "Why should Purdue develop multiple online versions of Course X across its campuses? Why not develop a single version of the course and make it available to students throughout the system?" There was also efficiency from the point of view of students: "Why should students have to enroll at a different Purdue campus to take an online course and then later transfer the credit to their home campus? Why should a Campus A student's progress toward a degree be delayed for lack of a needed online course on Campus A when the equivalent course is readily available at Campus B?" Efficiency in transfer was also a consideration: A system-wide online course should ensure that a consistent, mutually agreed-upon body of knowledge is covered and hence remove any concerns about transfers. (Issues regarding the transfer of credit for the same course were not uncommon among the Purdue campuses.)

As provost, Sands had undertaken an initiative to promote cooperation and collaboration among Purdue's campuses and to help Purdue operate more efficiently as a system. He sponsored semi-annual meetings to explore and report on collaborative efforts among Purdue campuses. As an outgrowth of that initiative, Audeen Fentiman, an engineering professor who was serving as special assistant to the president, was assigned to explore how online courses could be offered at the system level. She worked closely with PEC at West Lafayette and with the distance learning units at Purdue Calumet, North Central, Statewide Technology, and Fort Wayne to develop a pilot program. (IUPUI was not included because it was under Indiana University administration.)

Two iterations of a systemwide pilot program were conducted, and many challenges were encountered. In fall 2014, 27 students enrolled in two system-wide course sections; in Spring 2015, 188 students enrolled in thirteen courses. Because nearly all the enrollments were PWL students taking courses from regionals, PWL's outlay for the program exceeded $100,000. The program was suspended in spring 2015. A progress report on the systemwide online project from the cochairs of the project's coordinating committee, Sadowksi and Beth Pellicotti of the Calumet campus, noted several "barriers" to offering courses systemwide (e.g., different instances of Banner across the Purdue system, lack of transparency about course equivalencies across campuses), but noted that the disparate financial models between West Lafayette and the regionals was the root problem in adopting the system model. Because the West Lafayette campus was orders of magnitude larger than the regionals, most of the enrollees in system-wide pilot courses were full-time PWL students. Under PWL's block tuition model, full-time students paid a flat tuition rate; generally, additional credit hours did not generate additional revenues to the West Lafayette campus. The regional campuses' tuition rates were determined by the number of hours a student enrolled in; consequently, students enrolling in online courses did generate new revenues. Under the agreed-upon financial model, the students' home campus would transfer $200 per credit hour to the campus providing the instruction. This meant that PWL would incur a substantial cost for its students to enroll in system-wide courses, and regionals would benefit financially. Moreover, the transferred $200 per credit hour was less than the tuition their own students paid, so the regionals were losing money on systemwide students. At West Lafayette, PEC was paying departments $5,500 to $8,000 per online course section to defray their costs; under the system-wide course model, PWL would pay $12,000 to enroll twenty of its students in a system-wide course. This was the same scenario that caused PEC to step away from the Indiana College Network: it was more economical for PWL to produce our own courses than to enroll its students in a regional campus course or "system" course.

In their progress report, Pellicotti and Sadowski indicated that the pilot program did not establish a robust systemwide program of online courses, nor did it generate momentum toward systemwide offerings. "The possibility exists that Purdue does not need a large-scale system online program; however, the University will surely benefit from an agile, robust, right-sized system that can be accessed and used when the need for inter-campus offerings arises. We may not have that system fully developed yet; however, we are far closer to it than we were before the system-wide initiative." The report concluded by suggesting other areas in which the Purdue system's online initiatives might benefit from cooperation among its campuses.

The Provost's Advisory Group

On September 1, 2014, the university announced that Provost Deba Dutta (who had replaced Tim Sands when he became president of Virginia Tech) had established a Provost's Advisory Group on Digital Education and Environments, known by the acronym PAG DEE. The news release on the advisory group quoted Dutta on the need for such a group: "Purdue faculty have been engaged in online education for quite some time. They have brought innovations into the classroom and developed an array of new technology-based teaching and learning initiatives, making Purdue among the leaders in digital education. However, this is a field that is undergoing rapid change and therefore deserves continuous and increasing attention and investment" (Purdue News Service 2014a).

The PAG DEE was chaired by Sunil Prabhakar, professor and head of the Department of Computer Science. Other members were

- V. Ragu Balakrishnan, professor and the Michael and Katherine Birck Head of Electrical and Computer Engineering.
- Steve Beaudoin, interim associate vice provost and professor of chemical engineering.

- Jennifer Dennis, associate professor of horticulture and landscape architecture and agricultural economics.
- Rayvon Fouché, associate professor of history and director of American Studies Program.
- Timothy Newby, professor of curriculum and instruction.
- Sandra Sydnor, assistant professor of hospitality and tourism management.
- Michael Witt, associate professor of library science and head of the Distributed Data Curation Center.

Of this group, only Newby had substantial experience designing and delivering online education, as the coordinator of the College of Education's online degree program in education design and technology. No staff member of PEC was included in PAG DEE, nor were staff members of any other campus unit that was delivering online learning, such as Continuing Engineering Education. Instead, individuals actively engaged in online learning were interviewed by and provided documentation to PAG DEE members regarding their activities and policies.

Topics the PAG DEE was expected to advise the provost on included Purdue's "short- and long-term digital education goals, how best to engage digital education stakeholders on campus, and whether or not the campus was organized appropriately to deliver a high-quality and purposeful digital education" (Purdue News Service 2014a).

The PAG DEE report that appeared in spring 2015 did not aspire to fulfill all the provost's goals for the advisory group, but it laid the groundwork for such planning by providing an inventory of the campus's online programs and resources and exploring how eight peer universities managed online learning. The executive summary described the group's output as "a comprehensive overview of the philosophies and practices in online education at Purdue and at eight peer institutions." The group's reviews "surfaced important issues and questions for more in-depth discussion and investigation in the general areas of resources and support, policies and practice, and goals and execution." The report introduced its inventory of Purdue online programs by noting that it does not "pass any value judgments on any programs in this document, rather it is focused on providing an accurate (to the extent possible) snapshot of online activities at Purdue."

In July 2015 Mary Sadowski stepped down as dean of PEC and returned to her faculty role in Purdue Polytechnic Institute. Her tenure as dean had occurred as Purdue and the rest of academe experienced the "disruption" of online education, when universities came to understand how fully online education could transform higher education in ways that were both exhilarating (opportunity) and intimidating (tsunami). What had been a tangential enterprise at Purdue suddenly became viewed as a critical element in the university's future. As such, online learning attracted the attention of the trustees, two provosts, and a new president, all of whom became engaged in various ways. Prior to that moment PEC had been the focal point of online learning, with support from the administration on an as-needed basis. It administered online learning courses and programs for nearly twenty years, operating within the scope of financial constraints, procedural challenges, and faculty/departmental interest. PEC had learned how to flourish in the margins, to make online education work within the framework of a residential, R-1 university. So it was probably not surprising that during this transitional period PEC was not fully realizing the institution's ambitions in online learning, which were large but ill-defined. Those ambitions would become clearer under a new director and would entail a stunning new initiative by the president.

8

2015–2019

In march 2015 it was announced that the reporting structure of the units in Purdue Extended Campus would be changing "to better serve audiences and align with other areas of the university that pursue similar goals." Under the new realignment, the following changes were implemented.

- Purdue's Conference Division became part of the Office of Engagement. Nick Bonora, the division's interim director, began reporting to Steve Abel, associate vice president for engagement. Abel became associate provost for engagement in January 2016. Senior Programs coordinator Mary Gardner also transferred to Engagement.
- All functions related to online learning became a unit called Digital Education. A director of digital education was to be announced at a later date and would report to Frank Dooley, vice provost for teaching and learning.
- All instructional technology and instructional design staff would report through the Office of the Vice President for Information Technology and CIO.
- Purdue Extended Campus employees who worked on calendaring services would report through the Office of Marketing and Media in the Office of Public Affairs.
- The PEC staff who reported through Business Services continued to do that.
- Mary Sadowski would return to her faculty position on July 1, 2015. From April to July, she would assist the provost in formulating a digital education strategy. (Purdue News Service, 2015a).

Vice Provost Frank Dooley presented the proposed changes to the PEC staff in a meeting shortly before the public release. Regarding the split of Conferences from PEC, Dooley coined the analogy of splitting a growing plant into two pots so that each could grow more robustly. But the split was challenging in many ways. The two units had been joined since the 1950s and their functions had been defined in many of the same executive memoranda. The units had shared a business operation, technical support, and a registration system. Previous proposals to move Conferences to Housing and Food Services had failed; Provost Sally Mason had indicated that Conferences was an academic enterprise and, as such, needed to remain in the purview of the Provost's Office. The migration of instructional technology and instructional design staff to ITaP meant that PEC would no longer have its own instructional design team, which had been built up under Sadowski. (It had grown, in part, by PEC's contracting the services of some of ITaP's instructional design team.) Concerns about access to IT support came with the migration of PEC's IT support staff under Robin Jones. Some of the required support was unique to PEC, such as ongoing maintenance of PREMIS, and some was time critical, such as solving technical issues arising during registrations for conferences. Business Office personnel worked on both conference and continuing education processes. On a practical level, PEC and Conferences still shared physical space in Stewart Center.

The changes also included a rebranding of PEC as Digital Education. The somewhat uncommon terminology for online learning may have followed Provost Dutta from his previous post at the University of Michigan where "digital education" and "digital learning" were part of the administrative vocabulary. Except for evening classes and senior programs, the department's portfolio of programs was either online or had significant online components, so with the migration of Conferences and senior programs, the new branding was a largely accurate reflection of the department's activity.

With respect to Conferences coming under the purview of Engagement, PEC under Pagano reported to the vice president for engagement Don Gentry with the rationale that its chief mission was to engage the public with Purdue education. Conference business had a history of building mutually beneficial partnerships with various groups and organizations across the state and nationally. So the fit there could be viewed as natural. Goal 3 of Engagement's strategic plan could have been written for Conferences: "Identify and deliver innovative programs and strategies to meet the informational, educational and technical needs of the current and emerging workforce, business/industries and communities/regions." The migration of the engagement executive from an associate vice president to an associate provost confirmed Conferences' place within the university's academic mission, per former provost Mason.

Steve Abel said, "This change is going to be beneficial to all involved (including employees and our students) because areas that had previously been part of Purdue Extended Campus are better aligned with other areas at the University. Purdue Extended Campus has a long, rich history of innovative programs and service to both students and off-campus audiences. This realignment will allow us to better serve everyone so we can continue to offer innovative and necessary programs and services well into the future" (Purdue News Service 2015a).

As of the 2019–2020 academic year, the Purdue Engagement Office included the following areas:

- Purdue University Conferences—Nick Bonora, director
- Senior Programs—Mary Gardner, director
- Purdue Ft. Wayne—Sean Ryan, director
- Metro Indianapolis—Barbara Alder
- Purdue Northwest—Tim Sanders, liaison
- Service Learning—Lindsey Payne, director
- Purdue Center for Regional Development—Lionel Beaulieu
- Purdue Extension—Jason Henderson, director
- Colleges and Schools—Lisa Duncan, director
- K–12 I-STEM—Jennifer Hicks, director
- Motorsports and M-STEM—Danny White, manager
- Community Relations—Mike Piggott, director
- United Way—Megan Eberly, director

On July 20, 2015, Jon Harbor was announced as director of digital education and associate vice provost for teaching and learning. This was a new phase of the ongoing evolution of continuing education into distance education. In this new role Harbor would "provide long-term vision and oversight of Purdue's digital education (online courses and programs), as well as leadership for undergraduate programs serving the entire campus. He [would] also have administrative oversight for the Entrepreneurship Center, Exploratory Studies, Learning Communities, Undergraduate Academic Advising, and Summer Session" (Purdue News Service 2015b).

Harbor came with unusual qualifications for the position. He was an accomplished professor in Purdue's department of Earth, Atmospheric, and Planetary Sciences, where he had served as head. He had also served in other administrative roles, including associate vice president for research centers and institutes, interim dean of the College of Science, founding codirector of Purdue's Discovery Learning Research Center, and first director of the University's Global Sustainability Institute. He had coauthored more than 130 journal articles, three books, and over thirty book chapters and conference presentations. Just prior to his appointment to Digital Education he had spent a year as fellow of the American Council on Education. He had also worked with PEC's lead instructional designer Chad Mueller to develop EAPS 120: Introduction to Geography, as a fully online and asynchronous course, taught in four-week and eight-week formats. The course was designed to accommodate very large numbers of students and was very successful in attracting them.

An Action Plan for Digital Education

In his presentation to the PEC staff during the interview process Harbor had stressed that if he were to be appointed director he would launch a comprehensive, campus-wide planning process for digital education. The Board of Trustees' appetite for such a plan had not been fully satisfied since 2012. Despite the coincidence of timing, the Provost's Advisory Group on Digital Education and Environments (PAG DEE) report described in the previous chapter did not recommend the specific changes in the structure of PEC that were enacted in the spring of 2015, but it did enumerate areas where a more coordinated approach to digital education would be needed. The report observed that "coordination of digital learning programs is necessary for assessment to ensure quality and scale," but indicated that Purdue programs tended to operate independently and that best practices were not necessarily shared. It noted that "a business model and processes are needed for sustainability of programs, accounting, record-keeping, and support" but found that Purdue online programs operated on various business models. It observed that "After goals and requirements have been defined, the university will partner with one or more solution providers," but it described several provider relationships that had already been created before clear institutional goals and requirements were established. The report concluded that "the landscape of digital education is complex and will require clear vision, planning, stakeholder involvement, and unity of purpose to navigate. This vision and planning are not in place, nor is there a unity of purpose."

PAG DEE's conclusion defines the gap into which Harbor's commitment to executing a campus-wide planning process stepped. Harbor accepted the position conditioned on having the administration's support to conduct such a process. Harbor and President Daniels agreed on a timetable in which a plan would be completed by January 2016, after which implementation would begin immediately. That Harbor had given himself just over five months to complete a campus-wide plan came as a shock to the Digital Education staff. Typically, an academic strategic plan would take a year or more to complete. But Harbor had a clear idea of what he wanted to do and confidence that it could be accomplished in the agreed-upon time frame.

Harbor did not want to produce the typical academic strategic plan that becomes an unread tome collecting dust on a forgotten shelf. He framed the project as an "action plan"—the Action Plan for Digital Education, or, as it was snazzily abbreviated, AP4DE. It would minimize the usual infrastructure of strategic planning and cut right to the chase—how to get things done. He envisioned an open process, actively soliciting input from as much of the university community as had an interest. This broad-based approach was aptly characterized in Harbor's descriptive document shared with the Board of Trustees and university administrators: "Because digital education touches every student, every instructor, and most administrators, and because it significantly impacts the University's teaching and learning mission, the development of a digital education strategy for the University should be a highly public, transparent process, one that every member of the campus community—students, faculty, administrators—is aware of and has an opportunity to contribute to."

AP4DE was unlike the typical strategic planning process that centered on the unit's leadership and perhaps the addition of a consultant, with some limited opportunities for input from select stakeholders. (PEC had conducted strategic planning in this model during President Jischke's planning/metrics-driven administration.) In addition to a grassroots, bottom-up process, Harbor wanted the AP4DE process to model the best features of digital learning and thereby strengthen the campus concept of what can be accomplished intellectually in a technology-supported, cooperative environment. Toward that end, the open sessions were built on the "flipped classroom" model wherein registrants were provided with background readings and videos on the AP4DE website so that sessions could be devoted almost exclusively to discussion and not centered on presentations. (In a participant survey, 83 percent reported reviewing part or all of these materials.) Finally, he also wanted the process to build awareness and excitement about digital education on a campus that had been slow to buy in.

The process was key to the success of the endeavor. It would begin with open sessions that anyone in the campus community with an interest could attend. These would gather input on points of interest from the community. The sessions would be built around tabletop discussions among participants addressing some broad questions. Input from the discussions would be electronically captured via Hotseat, Purdue-developed software, and projected in real time on a large screen. Based on input from the general sessions, topics for more focused sessions would be developed. Focused sessions would operate in a similar manner to the general ones, but it was expected that attendees would probably have a special interest in the topic at hand. Input from the focused sessions would be captured and analyzed by the DE team. Harbor engaged Rab Mukerjea, who had served as the lead strategic planner under President Jischke, to develop and draft the written AP4DE plan.

The shaping of the report would be monitored by a select Coordinating Committee from across the campus community. Per Harbor's letter inviting members, the committee members would

- participate in some of the fall open and focus meetings;
- identify campus or external expertise we can draw on to inform the planning;
- provide perspectives on the input from the meetings;
- give feedback on drafts of the action plan and implementation plans.

Members of the Coordinating Committee included

- representatives of digital education stakeholders such as Center for Instructional Excellence (Chantal Levesque-Bristol), Libraries (Tomalee Doan), ITaP (Jason Fish), and the Graduate School (Linda Mason);
- representatives of online academic programs or courses such as John Fassnacht (Krannert); Kathryn Brownell (History); Tim Newby, Carla Johnson, Jennifer Richardson (Education); Natasha Watkins (Human Development Family Studies);
- leaders of the Provost's Advisory Group on Digital Education and Environments, Steve Beaudoin and Sunil Prabhakar;
- presidents of the student body and the Graduate Students Association.

Two identical general sessions were held in early October in the Discovery Learning and Research Center. Roughly fifty people participated in each in person. Several others participated online. The sessions were built around three twenty-minute tabletop discussions on three broad questions:

1. What key themes in digital education should be included in our action plan?
2. For one of these themes, what is a vision for the future we should work toward?
3. What needs to happen to achieve this vision?

After the sessions, participants could post additional thoughts through a Qualtrics survey on the AP4DE website. Table discussions were lively, and the input was rich and thoughtful.

Three themes emerged from the general session input as subjects of focused sessions in late October and November. The focal themes were

- support for digital education teaching and learning;
- quality, effectiveness, and affordability of online instruction;
- broadening access through digital education.

Focus sessions were structured like the general sessions. Attendance was comparable to the general sessions, with several people attending all or multiple sessions.

As input from these sessions was being processed the plan began to be assembled by Mukerjea with drafts and issues reviewed and discussed by the Coordinating Committee in regular meetings. By mid-December, a completed draft agreed upon by the Committee, was released onto the AP4DE website, and a final open session was scheduled for January 13, 2016, to allow the campus community to respond to the plan. Faculty and staff could also respond to the plan online via a Qualtrics survey. The survey and the session were structured around three questions:

1. What do you think are the most important or useful elements of the plan?
2. What elements of the plan do you feel are of lesser importance or could be eliminated?
3. What have we left out or overlooked?

Group discussion by forty-five participants in the open session produced ninety-eight separate input entries through Hotseat. The fourteen staff and faculty members who completed the Qualtrics survey submitted thirty-four discrete responses. These responses were considered by Mukerjea and the Coordinating Committee in January and February, adjustments were made, and a final plan was issued in late February. Senior university administrators approved the plan.

In keeping with Harbor's commitment to produce a report that was lean and digestible, the plan was only six pages long in its final form. As the term "action plan" implies, its core was six Key Action areas:

1. Launch an integrated support program for digital education that includes:
   a. instructional technologists, instructional designers, compliance and assessment specialists, DE pedagogy researchers;
   b. a coordinated center for supporting digital accessibility needs;
   c. a robust DE platform, and templates to provide a familiar and consistent environment for instructors and learners;
   d. a central repository of resources that facilitate best practice sharing and tool use development, including training for online learners and teachers;
   e. a 24/7 customer service help-line for teaching/learning communities;
   f. ongoing assessment and evaluation to inform program improvement, innovative pedagogical research, resource utilization, and future investments;
   g. an organizational structure that enables DE activities with creativity, agility, and effective and efficient coordination;
   h. a DE budget model that allows faculty and departments to benefit from launching and growing programs that are a good investment for their unit.
2. Create a central portal for digital education (DE) at Purdue University that will serve as a comprehensive gateway to all aspects of DE at Purdue, including:
   a. opportunities for learners (training, MOOCs, certificates, degrees);
   b. a one-stop shop for resources and training for instructors;

c. a showcase to highlight evidence- and research-based best practices;
d. resources and incentives for DE research, DE teaching/learning, and the DE community.
3. Support growth of an empowered university-wide digital education community. This would involve creation of DE Fellows in each college and facilitation by an agile organizational structure as well as resources matched to growing DE community needs.
4. Provide university/college awards/recognition in digital education. Develop a set of innovative incentives and awards for the scholarly engagement and delivery of digital education.
5. Create college-level digital education teams that include DE Fellows to coordinate and share resources across colleges, to share discipline-specific resources, and be the go-to person for faculty, and college-specific instructional designers.
6. Explore a "Purdue for Life" platform, a diverse and comprehensive portfolio of DE educational opportunities that can be accessed each time a person has new learning goals—alumni (degrees, certificates, corporate training programs, interests, NeXT, badges), current students (online courses, training programs, certificates), and future students (MOOCS, prep courses, dual credit).

These Key Actions were assigned to six implementation teams who developed implementation plans during the Spring 2016 term and succeeding terms. The path of digital education took some surprising turns in the next years, about which more will be said. Implementation of AP4DE was not as straightforward as anticipated and was accomplished by unexpected means. Much time has been devoted here to the AP4DE process because it modeled a means by which a conservative university could be engaged in a transformation that might have been impossible had it not been conducted in such an open and transparent fashion. For AP4DE the process, as much as the plan, was the message.

Funding for Digital Education

Even before the AP4DE process concluded, Harbor recognized that for the goals of the plan to be accomplished Digital Education would need a more consistent and larger revenue stream. Programs administered through DE had a variety of revenue models based on negotiated fees. Many departments had built up internal resources to manage administrative tasks that could be handled by a more robust central function. Departments used market-based fee structures, so some flexibility existed on the revenue side. On the undergraduate side, a key academic integrity element was missing: online monitoring of exams. Several private providers had developed robust systems to provide such monitoring, but at a significant per-student-per-exam cost. Pilot programs with different providers had begun, but the University had provided no central funding to cover the costs of this important service on an ongoing basis. Harbor and the DE administrative team began to work with Senior Vice President and Assistant Treasurer Jim Almond and other university financial administrators to develop the financial resources for Digital Education to provide the range of services identified in the AP4DE plan.

Ultimately the proposal arrived at was a digital education support fee of $50 per credit hour for graduate-level online degree programs and a $15 per credit hour proctoring fee for all graduate and undergraduate online courses. Almond's memo to the Board of Trustees' Financial Committee requesting authorization explained the digital education support fee as being "designed to fund the development of a robust and scalable campus-wide support infrastructure in Digital Education for online graduate programs. This can grow to include market analysis, financial analysis, program and instructional design, instructor training, program launch, marketing, recruitment, student success coaching, assessment, and analytics."

Almond's memo also indicated that some of the services provided by Purdue's Online Program Management partner (Wiley Education, formerly Deltak) could be provided by an expanded Digital Education at a rate far less than the 50 percent of gross charged by Wiley. Regarding the proctoring fee, Almond's memo explained that "fully online graduate and undergraduate courses, in which students are not required to come to campus, need online proctoring so that faculty can feel confident that their students are indeed the individuals taking their exams." The request was discussed at the BOT Financial Committee meeting of December 16, 2016, and approved.

MOOCs and FutureLearn

By 2016 the MOOC craze of 2012 had settled into a well-established role for MOOCs in higher education. The massive one-off MOOCs that attracted participants in the six-figure range had faded because of the overhead to mount them and the lack of revenues to cover expenses. Moreover, the prestige associated with attracting thousands to a MOOC diminished as large enrollments became more commonplace and didn't ultimately lead to programmatic gains. Also, completion rates in MOOCs were abysmally low, and institutions began to question how much learning was being accomplished in them. Universities looked for ways that MOOCs would not be an end unto themselves but as support for delivering academic credentials in an online environment. Since MOOC participants were predisposed to learning online, why not use MOOCs to attract online students into revenue-generating credential programs? One such approach was to offer a sequence of MOOCs around a subject area and grant academic credit for the verified completion of the MOOCs for participants who matriculate into an academic program. (Purdue's online communications masters experimented with this approach with some success.) Another integration of MOOCs into academic programs was to use them as the platform for instruction, thereby allowing degrees to be offered at a high volume and a lowered cost. In 2013 Georgia Tech announced a partnership with AT&T and the MOOC platform Udacity to deliver an MS in computer science on a massive scale for a total tuition of less than $7,000. The University of Illinois partnered with Coursera to offer an online MBA on a similar model.

A major concern about the incorporation of MOOCs into academe was the "high-volume, low-touch" model that had enabled them from the outset. This model minimized interaction of learners with instructors, and instruction was often recorded lectures with enhanced production values.

In early 2016 Harbor initiated discussions with a British provider called FutureLearn that had taken a unique approach to MOOCs. It was a spin-off company from Britain's Open University that had been delivering academic programs to working adults since 1969 using televised courses and the traditional British tutorial approach. Starting in 2013 FutureLearn was Open University's venture into online with a global focus. In addition to Open University's pedigree and history with nontraditional learners, FutureLearn brought with an online education model it called "social learning pedagogy" that was based on extensive educational research. It built into its courses extensive opportunities for students to interact and learn from each other. Scale became a vehicle for a diversity of experiences and cultures. FutureLearn encouraged instructors to present content as if they were speaking directly to individual students. It encouraged the structuring of courses as "storytelling" with a clear narrative progression to the resolving of an intellectual question. In short, FutureLearn was trying to create a "high-touch" environment at a high volume.

FutureLearn had over five million registered learners in countries across the globe as well as a network of seventy-five partner universities in the UK, Europe, Asia, and Australia. And FutureLearn was eager to have Purdue as a part of its first cohort of US partners that would include American University, Colorado State University, Penn State University, University of California–Berkeley, University of Chicago, and University of Virginia's Darden School of Business.

After a months-long contract negotiation, Digital Education began its involvement with FutureLearn by inviting four ITaP instructional designers to join four faculty members who had committed to develop FutureLearn courses to a two-day training at FutureLearn headquarters in London. In his invitation to selected faculty members Harbor framed the proposition by stating

> I am looking for the first four faculty members interested in potentially developing a MOOC on [the FutureLearn] platform—and more specifically to do this in a way that matches the Action Plan for Digital Education strategy: "to develop an intro MOOC (with DE badge) that is a module within an existing introductory course, so that the global audience (including potential new students and alumni) can interact with Purdue students in learning and discussions, and so that Purdue students can interact with the wide range of perspectives of a global community"

The idea here is that the MOOC becomes an exciting and regular part of a course instructors normally teach, rather than a completely separate task.

The training occurred over October Break, and the courses would be developed by instructors and instructional designers in the following months with the first offerings in April 2017 and then repeated. The courses in the initial offerings were as follows:

> *Communicating Complex Information: Presenting Your Ideas Clearly and Effectively*, Melanie Morgan, Brian Lamb School of Communication
> *Persuasive Communication: What Makes Messages Persuasive?* Bart Collins, Brian Lamb School of Communication
> *Time Management Strategies for Project Management*, Jun Fang, Engineering Professional Education
> *Brain and Behavior: Regulating Body Weight*, Kim Kinzig, Department of Psychological Sciences
> *Introduction to R for Data Science*, Mark Ward, Department of Statistics

System-Wide Digital Education

Interest in digital education was not, of course, limited to the West Lafayette campus. Online activities were growing on all Purdue campuses and doing so quite independently from each other. Consequently, there was competition among campuses in some domains and significant differences in how online learning was processed and supported across Purdue's campuses. Because the campuses fall under the purview of the provost, the Provost's Office asked Harbor to coordinate a digital education summit meeting among the campuses in the fall of 2016. Digital Education assembled and distributed a short survey of DE activities on the campuses. At the summit each campus was given the opportunity to describe its DE programs, and then, following the strategy of AP4DE, the session broke into table discussions of possible areas of cooperation that had been identified in the survey. These were

- shared technology
- online student orientation
- common training and development for online instructors
- system-wide online courses
- shared programs
- international study

After the summit, Harbor and Digital Education were tasked by the Provost's Office with identifying areas in which progress could be made in collaboration across campuses. Given the campuses' experience of trying to coordinate the joint offering of online courses described in the previous chapter, there was little appetite for pursuing shared courses or programs in the immediate future. Based on discussions at the summit, Digital Education's report suggested three areas where progress seemed possible:

- system-level licensing of software and tools for digital education
- shared faculty orientation programs and common quality standards (based on Quality Matters)

- a common orientation to online learning for students

The report noted that "successful collaboration in these areas might prepare the ground for more ambitious undertakings, such as making the technological and policy infrastructure consistent across campuses and offering online courses and degrees at the system level."

In the late fall 2017, the Provost's Office established a task force to explore these potential areas of cooperation to be cochaired by Harbor and Cassandra Boehlke of Purdue North Central. Groups representing each of the campuses were formed to develop a framework for action on each of the three areas. The groups convened in person three times between December and March, but groups did much of their work via teleconferences. Final reports were submitted late in the spring 2017 term, and a second all-campus summit was planned for September at which recommendations would be presented and discussed.

The instructor training group recommended that

- campus-based instructor training be maintained, but a system-level program be added to supplement it;
- a system-level instructor credential be delivered at the campus level;
- a system-level facilitation-only certification for adjuncts, limited-term lecturers, and graduate teaching assistants be established;
- a system-level quality certification for online courses be established;
- system-level online instructional awards be expanded and system-level events for instructor recognition and professional development be created.

The group on system-wide coordination of purchasing digital education tools and software observed that campus systems had different needs, so some purchasing would have to be done at the campus level and some could be done at the system level. The group advocated for a system-wide committee to explore the requirements of learning management systems. The student orientation group recommended that a system-wide online course orienting students to learning in a digital environment be created, required of all students enrolling in online courses or programs.

Many changes in the Purdue campus system had unfolded in 2017, including the combining of the North Central and Calumet campuses into one administrative entity, the transition of the Fort Wayne campus from joint administration by Purdue and Indiana Universities, and the addition of a new element into the Purdue system, which became the focal point of the fall 2017 all-campus summit and much else.

Purdue's Giant Leap

On April 27, 2017, Purdue president Mitch Daniels distributed an email to all faculty and staff announcing that Purdue was in the process of acquiring the academic assets of Kaplan University, a large, for-profit online institution with thirty-two thousand students, fourteen campuses and learning centers, and twenty-one hundred employees. Kaplan would become an independent, public, nonprofit university within the Purdue system. In a video that accompanied the email, Daniels presented the rationale for this surprising arrangement (available on YouTube at https://youtu.be/_xe77ppqzBo):

> In 1862, Abraham Lincoln and his allies gave birth to a new kind of university. A land-grant university, that would for the first time in history expand higher education beyond the wealthy and the elites of society.
>
> At Purdue, we try and never lose sight of our land-grant mission. We were put here to spread the benefits of higher education to all. . . . There are tens of millions among us without the postsecondary education that's now so necessary to a successful life. We cannot honor our land grant mission in the twenty-first century while ignoring the needs of these working men and women.

Daniels saw online education as the means to reach those who have been left out of traditional higher education, but Purdue currently lacked the needed skills to do so:

> A university like ours will be at risk if it drifts into the future without first-rate digital skills. Purdue today has only minimal online competencies. We have just a few online graduate programs and after a rigorous and candid analysis, we face the fact that we cannot build the capabilities we need to bring undergraduate degrees to those whose life circumstances will never fit our current on-campus offerings. We cannot truly fulfill our land-grant mission unless we acquire these capabilities, and I'm pleased to inform you, we have found a way to do so.

The vehicle for Purdue to accomplish its land grant mission would be Kaplan:

> We've identified an online education leader of high reputation, high integrity, and proven quality and expertise when it comes to serving working adults. Our trustees today have authorized its acquisition and conversion to a nonprofit public university.... The great challenge of bringing higher education to the missing millions and the surge of online education are going to be two of the most important phenomena in higher education over the next couple decades. We intend that Purdue be a leader in both.

The announcement took academia by surprise, but Harbor had seen something coming for some time. In his 2016 presentation to the Board of Trustees, he was asked for an estimate of how long it would take for Purdue West Lafayette to be in a position to offer fully online undergraduate degrees. (PWL academic administrators had been canvassed regarding their plans for online learning and none had indicated plans for an undergraduate degree.) Harbor answered five years. This time frame prompted President Daniels to explore other options. PWL had been successful in growing online graduate programs, because these typically involved courses in only one department, whereas an undergraduate degree involved courses from many different departments, all of which would have to agree to offer some fully online courses that would be open to students who would not be resident on the campus. In a traditional residential university, this is a major change in thinking, and managing that change is a slow process. As it selected courses to fund for online development, Digital Education gave additional weight to courses that could meet requirements for a variety of degrees, but expanding access to those courses to off-campus students would be challenging. In a "build or buy it" scenario, building appeared to be a very slow option, so President Daniels began looking for an option to acquire a fully functioning entity with significant existing undergraduate enrollment.

After the Kaplan acquisition, it was determined that PWL would not pursue fully online undergraduate degree programs, which would be a primary focus for the former Kaplan. PWL would continue to grow excellent, selective graduate online degrees, certificates, and noncredit courses.

Several senior leaders, including Harbor, had been aware of the arrangement before it was announced but had signed nondisclosure agreements because of Securities and Exchange Commission (SEC) rules surrounding the acquisition of part of a publicly traded company. Daniels had formed the deal working primarily with an inner circle of business and legal administrators. The Faculty Senate had not been apprised in advance because of SEC rules and senators expressed reservations about the way the acquisition had unfolded. The deal drew attention throughout the national academic community. The *Chronicle of Higher Education* wrote, "With a surprise deal to acquire the for-profit Kaplan University ... Purdue University has leapfrogged into the thick of the competitive online-education market." The purchase "puts Purdue in position to become a major force in an online landscape increasingly dominated by nonprofit institutions." (Blumenstyck 2017). *Inside Higher Education* called the acquisition "an unexpected tectonic shift in American higher education, revealing both the changing roles of public universities and the dwindling fortunes of for-profit colleges" (Fain and Selzer 2017).

The thirty-year agreement included a complex business plan that won't be elaborated here but seemed to protect the fiscal interests of Purdue. Having the approval of the Board of Trustees, the arrangement still needed approval from the Indiana Commission for Higher Education and Purdue's accrediting body, the Higher Learning Commission. On March 5, 2018, HLC announced that the new entity had been set on the path to accreditation. What had been dubbed "New U" during the announcement and approvals phases was named Purdue University Global and branded as Purdue Global. Purdue's new path for digital education was set.

Associate Vice Provost Frank Dooley oversaw the transition of Kaplan University into a new university within the Purdue system. Up to this point the Purdue system had consisted of multiple campuses under a single set of trustees, and with a single graduate school. Purdue Global would be a separate university, with its own board of trustees (though with some overlap with the existing Purdue board) and its own policies and procedures. Harbor worked with Dooley and others to enable the successful launch of the venture.

On March 30, 2018, Jon Harbor announced to the Digital Education staff that he had accepted a position as executive vice president and provost at the University of Montana. On his departure, Executive Vice President for Information Technology Gerry McCartney was named Executive Vice President for Purdue Online, the successor unit to Digital Education. In March 2020, Frank Dooley was named chancellor of Purdue University Global, and in August 2020, Jon Harbor returned to Purdue as Purdue University Global's provost.

Conclusion

In the modern age of adult education (1950s to the present), the media, libraries, and television remained important agencies of informal learning. More recently, independent study and online education have become very popular for those seeking additional information and training. In the 1970s, new terminology was introduced: "lifelong learning." Lifelong learning did not replace adult education. Instead, it became a new domain under the realm of adult learning (Stubblefield and Keane 1994, 304).

Today, higher education is on the verge of major changes. Many employers have made clear that their top priority is relevance to the rapidly changing workplace. Artificial intelligence, blockchain, virtual reality, and other technologies are driving these changes (Schroeder 2019). As a result, professional and continuing education divisions are moving from the periphery to the center of universities, pushing continuing education leaders to stay on top of these key trends.

Continuing education and conferences needs are now substantially more complex than in previous decades. Implementing virtual programs and global solutions presents new challenges. Scientific advances and emerging technologies offer new opportunities for clients and customers, while also posing new risks and demands. Meeting tomorrow's conference and continuing education needs will require combined expertise, perspectives, and resources. More than ever before, there is a need to look toward the future to anticipate potential needs. Conferences and Continuing Education departments must establish clear priorities in order to prepare themselves so that they can address these needs with integrity, professionalism, efficiency, and innovation.

In the past, meeting spaces at university and academic venues were often overlooked by conference planners. However, planners have now become increasingly interested in using these esteemed settings to create exceptional meeting experiences. The International Association of Conference Centers recently posted the following ten reasons why academic venues are excellent conference locations (Cooper 2019).

- Location and accessibility
- Prestige
- Superior learning environment
- Diverse meeting spaces
- State-of-the-art technology
- Exceptional catering
- Quality accommodations
- Access to recreational activities
- Corporate social responsibility
- Cost effective

The COVID 19 pandemic, raging across the world while this monograph was being developed, posed significant challenges for both conferences and continuing education at Purdue and elsewhere. As institutions went into lockdown mode, many conferences were canceled, creating financial challenges for Purdue Conferences. Some meetings became virtual in an online environment. From our current vantage point, it is difficult to project when campus-based conference offerings will return to their former levels or what role virtual meetings will continue to play in the conference business. It would seem that universities like Purdue would continue to have a strong case to make as providers of higher learning in virtual meeting environments.

As for online education, COVID transformed nearly all US colleges and universities into virtual institutions for a time. In lockdown, face-to-face classes stopped abruptly, and courses were offered only online. This situation gave nearly all teaching faculty an experience of teaching online, but under the worst possible circumstances and with little opportunity to work with instructional designers to transform their classroom courses into effective online learning experiences. Some students complained online classes cheated them out of the collegiate experience they had expected and paid for. But the motivators that drove the movement to online education seem too strong to dampen its momentum, and the reality of pandemic conditions may inspire more institutions and learners to consider online as an alternative to on-campus education.

For more than a hundred years (under various departmental names) the Office of Continuing Education and Conferences at Purdue University has contributed significantly to the university's learning mission to attain and preserve excellence in learning through programs of superior quality and value in every academic discipline. Through its commitment to a lifelong search for knowledge and wisdom, Continuing Education and Conferences has helped create a learning environment characterized by enhanced faculty (and staff) involvement in advanced learning and training. Though much has changed—Continuing Education has effectively (and administratively) become online education, and Continuing Education and Conferences have gone their separate ways—there is no reason to believe that this core philosophy will change very soon.

References

Black, Don. 1990. "An Unnoticed Part of Lafayette," *Lafayette Journal and Courier*, February 6.

Blumensytck, Goldie. 2017. "Purdue's Purchase of Kaplan Is a Big Bet—and a Sign of the Times." *Chronicle of Higher Education*, April 28. https://www.chronicle.com/article/purdues-purchase-of-kaplan-is-a-big-bet-and-a-sign-of-the-times.

Brown, Donald. 1985. *Purdue Extension: Strategies for Renewal*. Internal report.

Burrin, Frank. 1970. *Edward Charles Elliott, Educator*. Lafayette, IN: Purdue University Studies.

———. 1988. *Continuing Education at Purdue University: The First Hundred Years*. Internal publication. https://docs.lib.purdue.edu/continuinged/1.

Bonhomme, Mary. 1988. "A Brief History: Distance Education through Continuing Engineering Education." *Distance Education Newsletter of Purdue University Continuing Engineering Education*. 1 (1): 1–2.

Carlson, Eugene. *1985*. "Colleges Alight in New Areas to Exploit High-Tech Market." *Wall Street Journal*, June 25.

Cooper, Mark. 2019. "10 Reasons Why Academic Venues Are Excellent Conference Locations." IACC Blog, March 13. www.iacconline.org/iacc-blog/10-reasons-why-academic-venues-are-excellent-conference-locations.

Danglade, James. 1990. *The Indiana Council for Continuing Education: Seventeen Years of Cooperative Outreach in Higher Education, 1974–1990*. Self-published.

Fain, Paul, and Rick Selzer. 2017. "Purdue's Bold Move." *Inside Higher Education*, April 28. https://www.insidehighered.com/news/2017/04/28/purdue-acquires-kaplan-university-create-new-public-online-university-under-purdue.

Norberg, John. 2019. *Ever True: 150 Years of Giant Leaps at Purdue University*. West Lafayette, IN: Purdue University Press, 2019.

Pappano, Laura. 2012. "The Year of the MOOC." New York Times, November 2. https://www.nytimes.com/2012/11/04/education/edlife/massive-open-online-courses-are-multiplying-at-a-rapid-pace.html.

Poulin, R., and M. Bouke. n.d. "History of State Authorization." Western Interstate Cooperative for Higher Education.

Purdue Exponent. 1985. "Director of Continuing Ed Sees Potential." August 26.

Purdue News Service. 1999. "Purdue Restructures for Lifelong Learning, Teaching Excellence." Press release, January 29. https://www.purdue.edu/uns/html4ever/1999/990129.Swain.lifelong.html.

———. 2002. "Purdue restructures continuing education and conferences." Press release, May 16. https://www.purdue.edu/uns/html3month/020516.Gentry.Pagano.html.

———. 2011a. "Purdue Goes the Distance for Off-Campus Education." Press release, March 7. https://www.purdue.edu/newsroom/general/2011/110307PaganoDistance.html.

———. 2011b. "Purdue Extended Campus Reflects Growth of Conferences, Continuing Education." Press release, March 23. https://www.purdue.edu/newsroom/general/2011/110323PaganoExtendedCampu.html.

———. 2012a "Sadowski to Lead Purdue Extended Campus." Press release, May 10. https://www.purdue.edu/newsroom/faculty/2012/120510SadowskiExtended.html.

———. 2012b. "Purdue Announces Global Online Education Initiative." Press release, May 11. https://www.purdue.edu/newsroom/general/2012/120511CordovaHubU.html.

———. 2014a. "Provost Advisory Group to Focus on Digital Education, Environments." Press release, September 16. https://www.purdue.edu/newsroom/purduetoday/releases/2014/Q3/provost-advisory-group-to-focus-on-digital-education,-environments.html.

———. 2014b. "Did You Know? Midwest Program on Airborne Television Instruction." Press release, October 9. https://www.purdue.edu/newsroom/purduetoday/didyouknow/2014/Q4/did-you-know-midwest-program-on-airborne-television-instruction.html.

———. 2015a. "Purdue Extended Campus Units to Undergo Administrative Changes." *Purdue Today*, March 24. https://www.purdue.edu/newsroom/purduetoday/releases/2015/Q1/purdue-extended-campus-units-to-undergo-administrative-changes.html.

———. 2015b. "Harbor Named Director of Digital Education and Associate Vice Provost." *Purdue Today*, July 20. https://www.purdue.edu/newsroom/purduetoday/releases/2015/Q3/harbor-named-director-of-digital-education-and-associate-vice-provost-.html.

Sparger, Elena. 2012. "President Sands and Panel Discuss Online Courses at President's Forum." *Purdue Exponent*, October 3. https://www.purdueexponent.org/campus/article_af22e2a0-0617-5a32-a73c-a8f81c6693a5.html.

Staff Reports. 2012. "Board of Trustees Examine Online Courses, Other Items." *Purdue Exponent*, October 12. https://www.purdueexponent.org/campus/article_bddb5baa-14a4-11e2-ab5c-001a4bcf6878.html.

Sadowski, Mary. 2013. "Purdue Extended Campus (PEC) Update." Presented to the Academic Affairs Committee, Purdue University Board of Trustees, April 4. https://earchives.lib.purdue.edu/digital/collection/bot/id/52850/rec/1294.

Schmitt, Karen. 1985. "New Director Restructures Continuing Education." *Purdue Exponent*, June 26.

Schroeder, Ray. 2019. "Five Key Trends for Professional and Continuing Education Leaders in the Next Five Years." *The Evolution*, March 11. https://evolllution.com/revenue-streams/market_opportunities/five-key-trends-for-professional-and-continuing-education-leaders-in-the-next-five-years.

Shipp, Brianna. 2018. "Radio Then and Now." *Purdue Exponent*, July 1. https://www.purdueexponent.org/campus/article_bbfc2278-7d72-11e8-8878-477701a4df10.html.

Stubblefield, Harold, and Patrick Keane. 1994. *Adult Education in the American Experience from the Colonial Period to the Present*. San Francisco, CA: Jossey Bass.

Topping, Robert. 1980. *The Hovde Years*. West Lafayette, IN: Purdue Research Foundation, 1980.

Acknowledgments

Tom Robertson

Much love to my wife (Pam) and family (John, Nancy, Kelli, and Kyle) for their encouragement to write this historical summary. I appreciated their continued support while working through and completing the project.

Thank you to Steve Abel and Nick Bonora for their encouragement and cooperation while preparing this historical account.

Many thanks to two additional Purdue faculty whose similar writings motivated me to complete this project: Allan D. Goecker, *The Agriculturalist*, and Jim L. Windle, *Ever Grateful*.

The accounts contained within are as accurate as my memory, notes, files, and newspaper and magazine articles can make them.

A special thanks to Mike Eddy, who edited my original manuscript and contributed information about continuing and digital education.

Thank you to Robin Bell and Camilla Lawson for their input in chapters 3–8.

Thanks to Marcus Mues and John Underwood for their help in securing photos of Stewart Center.

Sincere thanks to Purdue Libraries for their encouragement to complete the project and for their financial support.

A sincere thank-you to Purdue University. It was a daily part of my life for thirty-four years. To Purdue, I will be **Ever Grateful, Ever True!**

Michael Eddy

Thanks to my wife Bonnie for putting up with my extended bouts of staring at the computer screen while drafting and editing this document. I promise all the piles of yellowed Continuing Education documents on the desk will go back into drawers soon. Very soon.

Thanks to the directors/deans who reviewed and commented on drafts of the chapters we wrote about their administrations: Mary Sadowsky, Mark Pagano, and Jon Harbor.

Special thanks to Jon Harbor and Frank Dooley, who now run Purdue Global. They cornered me in my office one afternoon when Jon had just arrived on the scene in Continuing Education and, knowing I was of retirement age, talked me into staying on for another three years. Those were the most exciting years of my career. I wouldn't have missed them for the world.

Thanks to all six directors/deans I worked for. It was always great having you out in front, forging the path and absorbing the "slings and arrows of outrageous fortune" while we got things done in the background.

Remembering director Dick Forsythe who passed away in 2019. He gave Bonnie and me our starts at Purdue, was our boss for ten years, kept his horses at our farm, and was our great good friend. He served Purdue for fifty years.

Thanks to Tom Robertson who pulled me into this project and gave me free rein to ransack my paper files, the internet, and my memory. I think he probably paid for more lunches than I did.

Thanks to all our Continuing Education colleagues who kept things running—to the program managers, the conference coordinators, the business office clerks, the Calendar Office schedulers, the registration clerks, the instructional designers, the IT staff, and the secretaries. We asked a lot, and they always delivered.

Thanks to Justin Race at Purdue Press for including our monograph in the Purdue Archive project, to Katherine Purple for facilitating the process of making an e-book, and to Gary Hamel for copy-editing our manuscript to make it suitable for public consumption.

Appendix 1

Biographies of Deans and Directors

Frank K. Burrin

Frank K. Burrin was a native of Waveland, Indiana. He was a 1942 graduate of Wabash College in Crawfordsville, Indiana. He received his MS and PhD degrees from Purdue (his PhD dissertation centered on the life of former Purdue president Edward C. Elliott). He worked in continuing education at Purdue from 1954 until his retirement in August of 1984. His titles included: professor of higher education, director of the Division of Conferences and Continuation Services, associate dean of continuing education, and director of Continuing Education Administration.

Some of the innovations Burrin oversaw included:

- Development of the Restaurant, Hotel, and Institutional Management Institute.
- The Indiana Council for Economic Education, cosponsored by continuing education and the Krannert School of Management.
- He was instrumental in getting continuing education registration and financial records computerized.
- Frank established a classification system for conferences and short course activities in 1977.

Prior to joining the Purdue faculty, Burrin taught high school English for several years. In the community, he was active in the Lafayette Rotary Club and the United Way. He chaired the United Way community-wide fund drive in 1974 and served on the Board of Directors for several years.

Charles S. Elliott

Charles (Chuck) S. Elliott received his undergraduate degree in mechanical engineering in 1964 from the General Motors Institute at Flint, MI. He received his master's degree from Indiana University in 1966 and his doctorate from Michigan State University in 1972. Prior to coming to Purdue, Elliott was director of special projects in the college of engineering at Wayne State University in Detroit, Michigan. He also worked as the coordinator of engineering extension programs at Wayne State University from 1974 to 1979.

Elliott joined the Purdue staff in 1979 as assistant director of Continuing Engineering Education (CEE) and was later named director. He served in this role until 1985. In 1985, he was named director of Continuing Education Administration at Purdue. Elliott served in this position until leaving Purdue in 1989. He was also a faculty member in the College of Engineering at Purdue during this time.

Elliott left Purdue in 1989 to become the director of the Center for Professional Development at Arizona State University. He was a faculty member there as well. Elliott retired from Arizona State University in 2001 as Professor Emeritus of Engineering.

Richard O. Forsythe

Richard (Dick) O. Forsythe graduated from Shepherd College (now Shepherd University) in 1956 with a degree in English and communications. While a student at Shepherd University, Forsythe was active in the music and drama departments.

After graduation, Forsythe taught high school for a short time before accepting a position at Purdue University in 1958.

Forsythe began his fifty-year career at Purdue as the director of instructional broadcasting at the Purdue radio station, WBAA. At that time the station was heavily involved in the "School of the Air," which was a state program that provided programming for public schools. He was also a faculty member in the department of Communications at Purdue.

Later in his career at Purdue, Forsythe served as an administrator in the Center for Instructional Services and in Continuing Education Administration.

Forsythe retired from Purdue in 2008.

Philip H. Swain
Philip H. Swain came to Purdue University in 1963 as a National Science Foundation Graduate Research Fellow. He earned his PhD in electrical engineering at Purdue in 1970.

Swain was appointed Assistant Executive Vice President for Academic Affairs on January 1, 1999. In August, 2001, this position was retitled Dean, Office of Instructional Excellence and Lifelong Learning, and he served in this capacity until June 2002. Previously, he was director of the Office of Distance Learning at Purdue from April 1997 through December 1998, and he was director of Continuing Engineering Education from 1986 to 1997. In 1994 he received the Meritorious Achievement Award in Continuing Education from the Institute of Electrical and Electronics Engineers. He is a fellow of the American Society for Engineering Education.

Swain retired from Purdue on December 31, 2006, and lives in New Bern, North Carolina.

Mark A. Pagano
A native of Southern Illinois, Mark A. Pagano completed his BS in thermal and environmental engineering in 1979 at Southern Illinois University Carbondale as a first-generation college student. He earned his MS in thermal and environmental engineering at SIU in 1983 and completed his PhD in engineering science in 1992 at SIU. As an SIU faculty member, he earned teaching awards and conducted research on chlorine in coal.

In 1992 Pagano began a nineteen-year career at Purdue University, where he where he reached the rank of full professor and served in many administrative positions. He served as department head of Mechanical Engineering Technology in Purdue's College of Technology beginning in 1993. From 1996 to 2001, Pagano served as assistant dean and administrator of Purdue's Statewide Technology System, the college's statewide outreach system. In 2003, he became associate vice provost for engagement and dean of Purdue Extended Campus. His tenure in PEC is discussed in Chapter 6 of this monograph.

In 2011, Pagano accepted the position of provost and vice chancellor for academic affairs at Montana State University Billings. In that role he led the development of the university's strategic plan and was instrumental in planning and starting the funding drive for a new science building.

In 2015, Pagano became the fourth chancellor of the University of Washington Tacoma. Arriving during the campus's twenty-fifth anniversary, he launched a strategic planning process for the next twenty-five years. He promoted the urban mission of the campus, working to expand access to higher education and create an equitable campus for students, faculty, and staff.

In 2021, Pagano stepped down as chancellor to return to teaching as a professor of mechanical engineering.

Mary A. Sadowski

Mary A. Sadowski was dean of Purdue Extended Campus from September 2011 until July 2015, where she managed conference activities and online courses and programs across the campus. After her tenure in PEC she returned to the Polytechnic Institute (formerly College of Technology), where her primary role was working with faculty across the college to ensure their success.

Before her appointment as PEC dean she was professor of computer graphic technology and associate dean of the College of Technology. While in the college, Sadowski provided leadership for the college's strategic initiatives in undergraduate education and served as coordinator of accrediting activities and initiatives, scholarships, and enrollment management.

Sadowski took an active role in developing a university-wide component of Service Engagement and Learning to expand learner-centered, interdisciplinary, and experiential opportunities for students and promote personal growth, leadership, real-world problem solving, career development, and citizenship. She was also a member of the Purdue Discovery Learning Task Force whose primary task was to explore futuristic technologies and strategies for teaching excellence. Prior to becoming an associate dean, Sadowski was a full professor at both Purdue University and Arizona State. Her specialty was computer and technical graphics, and she taught a variety of courses including CAD, web design, animation, and creative thinking. Her research interests included concept inventories, enhancing visualization skills and creative thinking. She published over forty-five papers, presented over forty-five technical papers, twelve workshops, and four textbooks.

Jon Harbor

Jon Harbor joined Purdue Global as provost in 2020. Previously, he served as the provost and executive vice president for the University of Montana and as executive director of digital education and associate vice president for teaching and learning at Purdue University. Harbor champions teaching excellence and the expansion of quality online education to meet the needs of diverse learners. He is experienced in designing processes that help academic organizations develop and implement novel strategies for success, with a particular focus on access, innovation, and excellence.

At the University of Montana, Harbor oversaw academic and student affairs and, with his team, launched partnerships to develop new online programs, transitioned to a data-informed academic advising model, designed a new budget model, and encouraged pedagogical transformations through a teaching excellence initiative. He joined Purdue University as an associate professor in 1994 and was promoted to full professor in 2001.

Harbor was recognized with Purdue University's top awards for both undergraduate teaching and graduate mentoring and was inducted into Purdue's "Book of Great Teachers." He has served in a wide range of leadership positions at the university level, including associate vice president for research, dean of a college of liberal arts and sciences, founding/interim director of a global sustainability institute, and founding codirector of a learning research center.

Harbor was born in England and completed his undergraduate studies at Cambridge University and his PhD in geological sciences at the University of Washington. His research and education initiatives have been supported by grants from the National Science Foundation, the Environmental Protection Agency, NASA, National Geographic, and international science foundations. Harbor has served as a Fulbright Senior Scholar, an American Council on Education Fellow, and a European Union Marie Curie Fellow. In 2015, Stockholm University awarded him an honorary doctorate.

An effective communicator with varied audiences, Harbor is a frequent speaker at conferences, at academic institutions, and for community, business, and K–12 audiences.

Steve Abel
Steve Abel was named associate provost for engagement at Purdue University in January 2016. Prior to his appointment he served as associate vice president for engagement (2014–2016), associate vice provost for faculty affairs (2012–2014) and held various positions within the Purdue University College of Pharmacy including assistant/associate dean for clinical programs, head of the Department of Pharmacy Practice, and Bucke Professor of Pharmacy Practice (1996–2014). Abel received his BS (Pharmacy) and PharmD degrees from Purdue University and completed residency training at Mayo Medical Center. He completed an Academic Leadership Fellowship through the Committee on Institutional Cooperation in 2007–2008, and an inaugural Purdue University provost fellowship focused on faculty affairs in 2009–2010. Abel is passionate about student education, faculty/leadership development, mentorship, and community engagement.

His research focuses on the development, implementation, and evaluation of progressive pharmacy services, student enhancement of pharmacy practice, patient safety, and inter-professional collaborative strategies to improve the medication use process in any setting. Abel developed the only fully immersive USP 797-compliant virtual cleanroom (based on video game technology) used for student education. He led the team that implemented international collaboration between the Purdue University College of Pharmacy, Indiana University School of Medicine, and Moi University in Eldoret, Kenya. The Purdue-Kenya program, the most comprehensive international initiative associated within a college/school of pharmacy in the United States, is currently sustained by two full-time faculty members in Kenya.

Throughout his career, Abel has been an advocate for the advancement of post-PharmD training in Indiana. Since 1980 he has facilitated the growth of postgraduate training opportunities (residencies, fellowships) from one position to over seventy. Abel has also been a strong advocate for partnerships supporting engagement, education and discovery throughout the State of Indiana. He has a history of active service in various pharmaceutical organizations including the Indiana Pharmacists Alliance, American Society of Health-System Pharmacists, American College of Clinical Pharmacy, American Association of Colleges of Pharmacy, and International Pharmaceutical Federation.

Appendix 2

Executive Memoranda

What follows are examples of executive memoranda from Purdue University relating to the history and policies of conference and continuing education activities. Full copies of these documents may be found through the Purdue University Archives and Special Collections at www.lib.purdue.edu/spcol or through the Purdue website.

PURDUE UNIVERSITY
OFFICE OF THE PRESIDENT
EXECUTIVE MEMORANDUM No. B-47
(Supersedes Executive Memorandum No. A-254, Dated December 28, 1964)

March 15, 1977

To: Deans, Directors, and Heads of Schools, Divisions, Departments, and Offices

Re: Assignment of Responsibility and Authority for Conference and Short Course Activities Sponsored by Purdue University

GENERAL

As a State university and land grant institution, Purdue University bears a major responsibility for continuing education. This Executive Memorandum assigns academic, administrative, and fiscal responsibility for all conferences and short course activities sponsored by a school, department, or other agency of the University and outlines those University-wide policies and procedures that govern the conduct of these activities. Exceptions to the policies and procedures presented in this memorandum must be approved in advance by the President or designee.

The term conference is used to denote an educational program of short duration (one to four days) sponsored by a school, department, or other agency of the University. Short courses are basically extended conferences (usually five days or more). These are not for credit and are primarily for part-time students. Conferences and short courses normally involve off-campus participants and are planned and orderly series of educative experiences designed to achieve one or more of the following objectives:

1. To update or expand technical or professional skills; or

2. To increase understanding of or involvement in special problems; or

3. To change attitudes or insights; or

4. To provide information about new techniques; or

5. To search for solutions to existing problems; or

6. To achieve learning for cultural enrichment.

In this memorandum the term "sponsor" is used to designate the academic school, department, or other agency of the University that assumes responsibility for the content and/or academic quality of the event. Every event will be sponsored by an academic school, department, or other agency of the University and all literature and brochures will indicate the sponsoring agency. Events may be conducted "in cooperation with" (non-financial assistance) or may be "supported by" (financial assistance) outside agencies provided there is internal sponsorship.

Responsibility and Authority for Continuing Education and Conference Activities

POLICY VIII.2.1
Volume VIII, Teaching, Research, and Outreach
Chapter 2, Conferences
Issuing Office: Provost
Responsible Officer: Directors, Continuing Education Division and Conference Division
Responsible Office: Continuing Education and Conferences
Originally Issued: March 15, 1977
Most Recently Revised: June 30, 2006

Table of Contents

Table of Contents	1
Statement of Policy	1
Reason for Policy	3
Who Should Know This Policy	3
Related Documents	3
Contacts	3
Definitions	4
Exclusions	5
Procedures	6
Responsibilities	11
History	12

Statement of Policy

As a state university and land grant institution, Purdue University bears a major responsibility to provide continuing education, professional development activities, and other extended accesses of learning and discovery to the public. This policy assigns academic, administrative, and fiscal responsibility for all continuing education and conference activity sponsored by a college/school, department, or other agency of the University. It also outlines those University-wide policies and procedures that govern the conduct of these activities. Exceptions to the policies and procedures presented must be approved in advance by the executive vice president and treasurer and the provost, or their designees.

Reason for Policy

Continuing Education
The general purpose of Purdue *continuing education* activities is twofold: 1) to extend the reach of Purdue learning to nontraditional learners beyond the campus, and 2) to increase flexibility and access to learning for traditional and nontraditional students on campus. To meet these goals, continuing education activities may take the forms of distance learning courses and programs, off-campus courses and programs, on-campus evening and intensive courses, educational/informational products, or contract training. These activities are distinct from the regular campus-based learning activities of the University in one or more of the following aspects:

APPENDIX 2

SUPERSEDED BY B-47

PURDUE UNIVERSITY
LAFAYETTE, INDIANA
Office of the President

28 December 1964

EXECUTIVE MEMORANDUM No. A-254

To: Deans, Directors, and Heads of Schools, Divisions, Departments, and Offices

Subject: Assignment of Responsibility and Authority for Conference and Short Course Activities on the Lafayette Campus

As a State university and a land-grant institution Purdue University bears a major responsibility for the continuing education of adults. This Executive Memorandum assigns academic, administrative, and fiscal responsibility for all conference and short course activity on the Lafayette campus and outlines those policies and procedures that govern the conduct of these activities.

In this memorandum the term "sponsor" is used to designate the academic department or other agency of the University that assumes responsibility for the content and/or academic quality of the event. Every event will be sponsored by an academic department or other agency of the University and all literature and brochures will indicate the sponsoring agency. Events may be conducted "in cooperation with" (non-financial assistance) or may be "supported by" (financial assistance) outside agencies provided there is internal sponsorship.

The term "chairman" is used to designate the University faculty or staff member who is assigned by the Department Head to represent the sponsoring department or agency in the discharge of its responsibilities. The term "coordinator" is used to designate the University staff member who is assigned by the Director of Conferences and Continuation Services to represent the University in all matters related to the administration, organization, and management of conferences and short courses.

Responsibility and Authority for Continuing Education and Conference Activities (V.B.4)

Statement of Policy

As a state university and land grant institution, Purdue University bears a major responsibility to provide continuing education, professional development activities, and other extended accesses of learning and discovery to the public. This policy assigns academic, administrative, and fiscal responsibility for all continuing education and conference activity sponsored by a college/school, department, or other agency of the University. It also outlines those University-wide policies and procedures that govern the conduct of these activities. Exceptions to the policies and procedures presented must be approved in advance by the executive vice president and treasurer and the provost, or their designees.

Reason for Policy

Continuing Education The general purpose of Purdue continuing education activities is twofold: 1) to extend the reach of Purdue learning to nontraditional learners beyond the campus, and 2) to increase flexibility and access to learning for traditional and nontraditional students on campus. To meet these goals, continuing education activities may take the forms of distance learning courses and programs, off-campus courses and programs, on-campus evening and intensive courses, educational/informational products, or contract training. These activities are distinct from the regular campus-based learning activities of the University in one or more of the following aspects: (1) They may address audiences that are generally distinct from the traditional on-campus student and who may require special administrative handling or pedagogical strategies; (2) They may serve the University's engagement mission as well as the learning mission; (3) They may be offered and delivered in nontraditional formats (e.g., intensive, off-campus, on-site training, distance learning, etc.); (4) They generally operate outside traditional academic loads and are fiscally self-supporting, thereby requiring special financial procedures; (5) They may be miscellaneous learning, engagement, or discovery functions that require the unique services and/or facilities managed by the Continuing Education Division.

Conferences The term conference is used to denote a noncredit educational program or activity sponsored by a college/school, department, student organization, or other agency of the University. To differentiate a conference from a continuing education activity, in general, the administrative effort and resource cost for a conference are primarily related to the logistics and hospitality services for the event while the administrative effort and resource cost for a continuing education activity are primarily related to the instructional component. Conferences involve both on-campus and off-campus participants and are planned and designed to achieve one or more of the following objectives: (1) to update or expand technical or professional skills; or (2) to increase understanding of or involvement in special problems; or (3) to offer new attitudes or insights; or (4) to provide information about new techniques or disseminate new knowledge; or (5) to search for solutions to existing problems; or (6) to achieve learning for cultural enrichment; or (7) to conduct a business, social, or administrative function of a campus unit or outside organization that requires the unique services and/or facilities managed by the Conference Division.

https://www.purdue.edu/policies/governance/vb4.html

APPENDIX 2

Responsibility of Approval, Calendaring, and Scheduling of Facilities for University-Sponsored Activities (B-46)

(Supersedes Executive Memorandum No. A-222, dated 1 September 1962)
March 15, 1977

General

With the increasing demand made upon University facilities and with the space limitations the University faces, it is essential to have an all-campus calendar listing student, staff, and outside events. To reduce conflicts in scheduling of facilities and make the most efficient use of the available facilities, all student, staff, and outside events and activities will be calendared.

This memorandum establishes the University-wide policies covering the approval, calendaring, and scheduling of facilities and assigns responsibilities for implementing these policies on any Purdue campus. Any exceptions to the policies presented in this memorandum must be approved in advance by the President or his designee.

In this memorandum the terms "approval," "calendaring," and "scheduling" of facilities are defined as:

1. Approval: The laws of the State of Indiana have conferred upon the Board of Trustees the authority to govern the disposition of the property owned, used, or occupied by Purdue University and to make all rules and regulations required or proper to conduct and manage Purdue University. The Board of Trustees has authorized the President of the University to establish regulations governing the method and purpose of the use of University facilities. The President, in turn, has delegated this responsibility to certain offices, committees, and administrative officers. All activities and events conducted at Purdue University are to be "approved" by the proper office, committee, or administrative officer.
2. Calendaring: Certain types of activities and events will be listed, or "calendared," with the appropriate University office. The calendaring of activities and events essentially provides an information service.
3. Scheduling of Facilities: When specific space is reserved (with the administrative officer in charge of that facility) for a specific activity or event, that facility has been "scheduled." Scheduling than refers to the act of reserving facilities for a specific activity or event with the proper administrative officer.

https://www.purdue.edu/policies/facilities-safety/b-46.html

Compensation Policies for University Staff Members Participating in Continuing Education Activities (C-18)

(Supersedes Executive Memorandum No. C-18 dated April 1, 1991)
March 30, 1998

This memorandum outlines the general policies that apply to the compensation of Purdue University staff members when they participate in any activity administered by the recognized continuing education unit on any of Purdue's campuses. These policies shall apply on all Purdue campuses. Subject to the prior approval of the President, and within these general policies, specific additional policies may be developed for each campus.

It is the intent of these policies (1) to maximize continuing education programming and to extend options to all citizens of Indiana and elsewhere to pursue lifelong learning in a variety of formats within the educational mission areas which Purdue University is committed to serve; and (2) to provide a faculty-staff and/or departmental compensation system commensurate with the University's continuing education responsibilities; and (3) to maintain the financial viability of Continuing Education and its activities.

Continuing education programs may be considered in two major categories:

1. Academic credit courses, and
2. Noncredit activities.

Staff members participating in continuing education activities may be compensated by:

1. Regular Assignment: Staff members can participate in continuing education assignments as part of their regular school or department assigned load.
2. Extended Employment: Summer employment for academic-year employees is considered extended employment.
3. Additional Duties: Part-time staff members will be compensated for activities up to 1.00 FTE as additional duties. Activities beyond 1.00 FTE will be compensated as overload. Effort will be determined based on time involved in the continuing education activity.
4. Overload: An overload assignment provides compensation for services over and above the regular assigned load during the fiscal year for fiscal year staff, or the academic year plus extended summer employment for academic year staff.

https://www.purdue.edu/policies/human-resources/c-18.html

APPENDIX 2

Overload Compensation (VI.C.4)

(Supersedes Executive Memorandum No. C-18 dated April 1, 1991)
March 30, 1998

STATEMENT OF POLICY

On occasion, faculty and staff are asked to assume additional assignments that are reasonable extensions of their normal job duties. Compensation in addition to the normal salary and wages is not provided on these occasions. Unusual situations may arise that require faculty and staff to perform beyond the scope of their primary employment understanding. In these situations, Overload Compensation may be granted in accordance with this policy.

There are two instances in which it is appropriate to utilize Overload Compensation.

1. Effort exceeds normal load, non-emergency: The employee is assigned to and participates in an assigned activity that is clearly beyond the primary employment expectations, and the employee's appointment for the activity represents the most economical and/or strategic approach to meet the unit's need.
2. Effort exceeds normal load, emergency: The employee is assigned to and participates in an assigned activity that is clearly beyond the primary employment expectations, and alternative arrangements are not feasible. Every reasonable effort must be made to incorporate the activity into the regular duties and responsibilities of the unit before the use of Overload Compensation is recommended. Even after Overload Compensation is approved, the unit is expected to bring the activity into the regular pattern of assigned duties.

Payment of Overload Compensation must represent the best use of University resources, regardless of the funding source. Overload Compensation may not be used for sponsored project effort. Overload Compensation may not exceed 20 percent of the salary for fiscal-year employees or the equivalent amount of 25 percent of the base salary for academic-year employees.

https://www.purdue.edu/policies/human-resources/vic4.html#:~:text=Overload%20Compensation%20may%20not%20exceed,salary%20for%20academic%2Dyear%20employees

Appendix 3

Traditional Conferences, Special Interest Conferences, and Continuing Education

Sampling of Traditional Conferences Held Annually

- Pest Management Conference (84 years)
- Crop Management Workshops (32 years)
- Industrial Waste Conference (73 years)
- Greater Lafayette Science and Engineering Fair (70 years)
- Purdue Road School (106 years)
- Purdue Underground Corrosion Short Course (59 years)
- Multi-State Poultry Feeding and Nutrition Conference (over 30 years)
- 4-H Roundup (over 100 years)
- Multiethnic Introduction To Engineering, M.I.T.E. (45 years)
- Presbyterian Youth Triennium, PYT (over 30 years; held every three years)
- Annual Conference for Veterinarians and Veterinary Technicians (39 years)
- Civil Engineering Professional Development Seminar, CEPDS (35 years)
- Purdue Income Tax School (52 years)
- Top Farmer Crop Workshop (52 years)
- Indiana Bankers Ag Clinic (53 years)

Sampling of Special Interest Conferences with Unique Content and/or Speakers:

- 4-H Roundup: Special keynote speakers Bob Evans in June 1983 and Robert Keeshan (Captain Kangaroo) in June 1987.
- National Herb Growers Conference July 1988.
- Game Bird Cooking School March 1990.
- Big Bird Conference November 1993 (featured information on ostriches, rheas, and emus, along with a trade show).
- National Order of the Arrow Conference August 1994 (attended by 6,000 Boy Scouts).
- Indiana State MathCounts held at Purdue March 9, 2013.
- Junior Veterinary Camp (for grades 8 and 9) held at Purdue June 8–14, 2014.
- Senior Veterinary Camp (for grades 11 and 12) held at Purdue June 15–21, 2014.
- Hugh O'Brian Youth Foundation World Leadership Congress July 1997 (Actor Hugh O'Brian was an integral part of the meeting. He portrayed Wyatt Earp in the 1950s TV show *The Life and Legend of Wyatt Earp*).
- United Association of Journeymen and Apprentices of the Plumbing and Pipefitting Industry (UA) was held at Purdue (always in early August) from 1954 to 1989.

Sampling of Purdue Continuing Education

- Independent study classes began at Purdue in 1983.
- Courses offered via satellite and the internet began at Purdue in 1997. They were run through the Indiana Higher Education Telecommunications System (IHETS) and were followed with online courses starting in the early 2000s, with Distance Learning in 2010.
- Purdue Global was created in 2017 with the purchase of Kaplan University, and it continues to offer online classes today.

Appendix 4

Events of Interest Held at Purdue, 1974–2019

- Barry Manilow performed at Purdue July 6, 1985
- President Reagan spoke at Purdue April 9, 1987
- Former President Jimmy Carter spoke at Purdue February 11, 1991
- Sandra Day O'Connor spoke at Purdue January 25, 1995
- Kenny G and Toni Braxton performed January 11, 1996
- Purdue played in the Rose Bowl January 1, 2001
- Senator Bob Dole spoke at the Purdue Ag Alumni Fish Fry February 2, 2002
- Commercial airlines left the Purdue Airport February 15, 2004
- James Earl Jones spoke at Purdue October 3, 2008
- Captain Chesley (Sully) Sullenberger was honored at Purdue by Neil Armstrong November 12, 2010
- Madeleine Albright spoke at Purdue October 10, 2013
- Gene Kranz spoke at Purdue September 25, 2014 and July 18, 2019
- Condolezza Rice spoke at Purdue October 9, 2019
- A Purdue Astronaut Reunion was held on Homecoming Weekend October 10–13, 2019

About the Authors

Tom Robertson is a native of Oxford, Indiana. He received his BA, MS and Ed.S degrees from Purdue University. Tom worked in the department of Continuing Education at Purdue University for thirty-four years. He retired from Purdue's Conference Division in 2017, where he was a senior conference coordinator. He served as interim director of the Conference Division in 2009–2010. While working at Purdue, Tom was active in a number of professional organizations: University Continuing Education Association, Association of Continuing Higher Education, Indiana Association of Adult and Continuing Education, and Phi Delta Kappa. Prior to working at Purdue, Tom was a teacher in the Benton Community School Corporation from 1975 to 1983. While working within the Benton Community Schools he taught a GED Preparation Course, supervised several student teachers, served on numerous committees, and was a member of two NCA Elementary Accreditation teams. Tom and his wife (Pam) have two grown children, John and Kelli, along with four grandchildren. Tom, Pam, and their children (and spouses) are all Purdue alums. **Black** and **gold** runs deep in the Robertson family.

Michael Eddy earned his bachelor's (1972), master's (1976), and doctoral (1985) degrees at Purdue University. In 1986 he joined Continuing Education to manage its communications and marketing. In 1997 Eddy assumed administrative responsibility for evening classes, extension classes, distance learning courses and degree programs, senior programs, and travel courses. He served in leadership for the Indiana Council for Continuing Education from 1997 through 2000. He represented Purdue to the Indiana Partnership for Statewide Education from 1997 to 2013. The University Professional and Continuing Education Association recognized Eddy's career with its 2015 John L. Christopher Outstanding Leadership Award. In 2018, Indiana's governor recognized his service to the state with the Circle of Corydon award as he retired from a thirty-two-year career in Purdue Continuing Education.